THE 48 ACTS

LIVE YOUR LIFE IN A BETTER, DEEPER WAY

PADDY RAFTER

WWW.PADDYRAFTER.COM

To my wife Maura and my children Sean, Isabelle, Patrick and Alexander with love and gratitude.

CONTENTS

PART III
THE SIXTEEN FALSE BELIEFS

PART IV
THE SIXTEEN KEY ACTIONS

PART V
CONCLUSION

REALITY CHECK—THIS IS WHERE WE ARE NOW

Before you commence *the 48 Acts* and consider implementing and enacting the truths within, it is first necessary for you to examine the sixteen 'Acts of Desolation'. Why should you need to do this?

Everyone fits somewhere on the spectrum of desolation. This is how we are as humans. The important thing for you is where you are on that spectrum and how you have dealt with it heretofore. Reading the 'Acts of Desolation' and the accompanying preamble will bring you into some form of identification, giving you the beginning of a reality check. All that is necessary for you to do is read and identify as many times as is needed to absorb that which is relevant to you. This is your first great action, because you are identifying where you are, though you may only be able to do this after many repeated attempts. That is OK, that is how it must be.

What is it really like to feel total desolation? You feel like an empty, hollow shell. At best you're going through the motions: not living, but existing. It is a place beyond pain, beyond suffering, beyond hope or hopelessness. No motivation or joy, or happiness, or pleasure in any of the things that used to give you pleasure, or even some form of satisfaction or distraction. You might call it depression.

It is destruction of self and self-identification; it takes a long time to happen and is almost impossible to get out of.

The root causes are your own ignorance, your lack of self-empathy and self-compassion, and blindly thinking people will treat you the way you think you should be treated.

When your depression and apathy become chronic and you still don't know why—or even worse, you do know why, but you still feel you cannot do anything about it—then this is the pit of hell.

How can this happen to an individual? Furthermore, how can anyone embark on an extraordinarily destructive lifestyle or a life full of maladaptive behaviours and destructive thinking? How did you embark on this very same destructive lifestyle? If this applies to you, how did it happen to you? How has your life come to this point? How have you ended up the way you are? The answer is, very easily indeed.

How does it happen that you end up unable to feel or care about anybody, even those closest to you, or even yourself? That all your feelings are confused and undifferentiated? That you cease to look after yourself, or mind your health, or care what happens to you? That eventually your mode of survival is at best a joyless existence, where the ultimate survival tool is constantly playing with the idea that you will die shortly anyway, either by your own hand or by your indifference to your health and well-being? This is beyond a feeling of total hopelessness. You don't care if you live or die, and there is a pervasive feeling of utter worthlessness.

If you recognize this situation, or you can identify with it or some of it, then this book will help you.

So, it is worth repeating the question because you constantly, endlessly repeat this question in the movie in your mind. How did this happen, and what if anything can you do about it?

The circumstances will be different from case to case, but the main themes are readily identifiable and are pretty much as follows:

THE SIXTEEN ACTS OF
DESOLATION

1. You were brought up in a family, or a household or care environment, where you experienced trauma through neglect or abuse of some kind, be it physical, emotional, mental, sexual, or through indifference, minimization, or devaluing. This may have been done intentionally, or unintentionally through ignorance. Alternatively, you may equally have been brought up as spoiled and entitled, or overprotected. It is also possible that you have an incorrect perception that you were brought up in a cold and unloving environment, or that you were not respected or encouraged. Nevertheless, this is your truth. Unfortunately, the consequences are the same.

2. Because of this early experience, you craved acceptance and approval. However, in school you may have been bullied, ridiculed, and laughed at by fellow students, teachers, or both.

This reinforced your programming of feeling stupid, useless, and unwanted. At this stage you probably started acting out or being difficult just to gain attention.

You may, on the other hand, have been the complete opposite: the model student, extremely high achieving, with great talent of an academic, musical, or sporting nature. You excelled beyond all others, and you received validation. Your talent, in this case, becomes inexorably linked with your persona.

3. This pattern, once established, continues through every single facet of your life: school, college, marriage, partners and relationships, work, sport, and lifestyle.

4. Your life becomes intolerable, either through your own unrealistic expectations or the expectations of others, or because you are mired in an unlivable, destructive, addictive lifestyle. In response, you create coping strategies. Many of us will have created these coping strategies from a very early age. Unfortunately, these coping strategies, while they work well at the time for us, helping us to survive, become maladaptive behaviours if we carry them into later life.

5. You needed to get away from reality. The reality of the pain. The reality of being unable to cope and live in the world. You start to use and then abuse alcohol, drugs, or sex, or you adopt other maladaptive behaviours to take you temporarily away from your pain, the world, and reality. You join the ranks of the countless millions of people, who, unable to cope, resort to pain management in one form or another. Feeling that we did not get the approval and appreciation we desperately needed we sought other ways, other means to live a life without the proper blueprint for living we came to believe was missing. The instinctive plan to know how to live.

6. Many of you will now create an alternative universe, a fantasy world where people will treat you well and with respect. You live in this fantasy world because it is the only world in which we can feel valued. It becomes your refuge.

7. As life becomes ever more unlivable, you may become stuck in narcissistic relationships because you gravitate towards them, drawn inexorably by the promise of love for which you have searched all your live. You believe the narcissist will give love to you, but the narcissist only truly loves themselves, and will love you only on their terms. It may also be that you have been in a coercive controlling relationship for years, even from childhood, and the consequences of this terribly destructive relationship have led you on a path of self-destruction. You believe as you perceive. The damage caused by

living in a coercive controlling relationship is catastrophic as your self-image is destroyed. Everything seems unending, unrelenting, and hopeless.

Narcissists will love you as an extension of themselves, not for who you are, but then you will feel you deserve nothing better anyway and something is better than nothing. You have now become voiceless. You know that nobody will believe you if you tell them how it really is. You are now living in a nightmare. Alternatively, you hurt, damage, and destroy the lives of all those closest to you, not because you mean to, but because of your own unwellness, ignorance and despair.

8. Now your coping strategies are not working, and your short-term measures are making everything immeasurably worse, so that life is unlivable, and death is almost welcome. At this point, some of you develop last-gasp strategies such as apathy, cynicism, fantasy living, or indifference. You may develop a fear of caring because you have never had that care returned to you for who you are. If you are one of those fortunate enough to be loved just for you, well then you have probably destroyed that love through your actions anyway. You now have a fear of being loved. Eventually, you are unable to motivate yourself to do anything, to be anything, to feel anything, or to see anything.

9. You feel that you can't turn to God or his priest/pastor enforcers since He promises to love you on the one hand and condemns you to eternal damnation on the other. This is just another form of fear and control that you have experienced since you were a little child. And then as the final irony, He promises you that you will live forever as a reward—you who can't handle another day.

10. You are now at an existential crisis, and believe it or not, you are not alone. This is happening to millions of people all over the world, and in my experience, we are all too afraid to say it. We suffer in silent desperation.

11. It is not your fault. You have been blamed, chastised, minimized, and vilified often. You have lived and behaved badly as a response, confirming that which was thought of you. Alternatively,

you have driven yourself to the point of exhaustion trying to develop your talents to a stage of perfection which does not exist.

12. The world is also confirming the hopelessness and pointlessness of your and our accidental existence, as is science and the corporate media.

This is the new world epidemic, 'The Pandemic of Meaninglessness'. All our heroes, gods and truths are gone. Everyone feels lost, alone. You feel this is the time of your greatest crisis.

It is not your fault. By reading this, you will see that this is true. I understand because I have been there.

13. It is in our hour of greatest despondency and despair that the process of awakening can begin.

14. It is told, is it not? All the mystics, prophets, and seers agree that you must lose everything in order to find it, and this is very difficult. But you can only find your life by first losing it.

15. Here, you who have suffered so much have an advantage because you have already lost, and your loss can be turned to your great gain.

16. If you are prepared to wholeheartedly embrace the ideas in this book and embrace this way of life, then you can have a life as it should truly be lived. Despite all your past transgressions, real or imagined, and despite all the hurt you have caused or that may have been caused to you, yet still you can live a life of peace and happiness beyond your imagination. You will come to see and understand that there really is a force of love that permeates the universe.

You have paid the price for love, and you have paid the price for your indifference. You have paid the price for your programming, and you have certainly paid the price for the past in the most expensive currency of all: your shame and guilt.

It is in this very lowest point of your existence that you can see the chink of light, and if you can just grasp one iota of courage to change, to look and see, then you can live again in reality.

PART I

PART I

PROLOGUE
THE 48 ACTS

I am glad you are here. I am glad that you have begun to read *The 48 Acts*. It is my deepest hope that these 48 Acts will help you. They will help you to live your life in a better, deeper way. If you follow *The 48 Acts*, then you will be able to conquer your addictions, your unhappiness, and your depressions, and find a new way to live well.

I am sharing some things I discovered and have come to understand after fifty years of searching, studying, and suffering. My only and earnest wish is that by sharing this with you, the reader, and the listener, you may find some help on your path through life. I just ask that you keep an open mind as much as you can, at the moment. Please read the prologue and the chapters before the Acts as this is essential to give you a background both to the world and our place in it. Reading or hearing my story may help you to identify in some manner. Some of the things I did or that happened to me may resonate with your own story in some way. In time you will learn not to identify. What do I mean by this? Constant, repeated identifying with some trauma or pain in your past only reinforces its power over you. Examine it and own it, then move on. In time you will learn to convert your black and white, binary thinking into a new way of thinking. When you have begun to read the Acts themselves, listen to your own voice inside of you; do not accept anything I say because I say it but examine it carefully. I do not wish to proselytize, but to enlighten. To ease the burden.

To start, we must begin at the beginning.

Our planet formed 4.5 billion years ago, from a universe that is 13.8 billion years old. Life began on earth 3.7 billion years ago and the first bipedal hominid (human ancestor) walked the earth approximately five million years ago. Modern *Homo sapiens* (humans), through a process of continuous advancement, evolved into our present form between three hundred thirty thousand to approximately two hundred seventy thousand years ago.

Our evolutionary development from our common ancestor with the other primates has been an extremely slow, incremental process along a truly immense time scale. Our last shared ancestor with the other primates was at least six to seven million years ago. The rate of change in our development from the first hominids has been very gradual indeed. Each iteration of hominid development and its increasing complexity can be measured in million-year gaps, until we reach a million years ago. From that point until the present, each stage of our evolution has been an ever increasing process, taking less time than the preceding stage.

For example, it took us millions of years to develop bipedalism; we spent over a million years developing as hunter-gatherers even though we were not *H. sapiens* for most of the journey. We evolved through changes in our environment and circumstances, even to the point that we evolved into a different species. A common theme throughout our evolution is that we adapt and change to suit our conditions and to survive.

Approximately forty to fifty thousand years ago, at the time of the upper Paleolithic transition or shift, we began to evolve and advance ever more quickly. We built campsites, developed advanced tools, etc.., but we still lived a nomadic existence.

By the end of the last ice age, twelve thousand years ago, we had begun to form larger clans with linked structures to other clans or tribal groups. Within two thousand years we had formed the first semi-permanent settlements. We developed the first permanent human-made sites dedicated to communal worship before we developed permanent habitations. We developed the first city-states a mere seven to eight thousand years ago. We began to change and adapt more rapidly, beginning a sedentary way of life and leaving our nomadic past behind. We developed writing, agriculture, and much more advanced tools and culture.

Over the last five to six thousand years, we have evolved at a staggering rate. This is even more true when you compare the glacial progress of our early evolution with the extreme rapidity of modern evolution.

But even that pales in comparison to the rate of change in the past two hundred and fifty years.

Our industrial revolution began just two hundred and fifty years ago. The first practical automobile was developed by Carl Benz in 1886 and the first airplane was developed a mere one hundred and twenty years ago. Along the way we learned how to split the atom and make an atomic bomb in 1945. Nuclear bombs are now capable of wiping out our civilization in an instant. Nuclear power is also capable of supplying all our energy needs. It depends on how we use a new or existing technology, not on the technology itself. Now we have an advanced digital technological technology which really has taken just forty years to develop. Once again, it depends on how we use it.

Our understanding of science and our mathematical progress have also been exponentially fast. Our medical advances are unparalleled. The standard of living in most of the world is much higher than ever before in our history.

For two hundred and fifty years now, we have relentlessly driven onwards to achieve humanity's perceived goal of being 'bigger, faster, stronger'. This has obviously had positive effects, as we have seen with the great innovations in medicine, science, and technology.

Much emphasis has been put on the concept of driving and growing the cognitive and rational part of our brain. That has borne fruit with the obvious, superfast growth in technology and the many advances we have made. However, this progress, although it has brought great advances and great rewards, is not reality. It has come at an enormous cost.

The reality is that the development of our emotional and biological brain has fallen far behind the development of our cognitive/rational brain. We spend most of our day in our emotional brain, and this part of our brain is making most of our decisions. The big problem is that we do not realize this fact. We think we are making rational decisions with our cognitive brain only, not realizing there is another part of our brain at work at the same time. This is very important for us to understand.

In the most straightforward terms possible, here is what is happening in the modern human brain.

The human brain is split into two hemispheres, the left and the right. These two parts have very different functions and largely operate on an individual basis. They are connected by a band of nerves and fibers called the corpus callosum.

The left hemisphere controls comprehension, speech and writing.

The right hemisphere controls spatial awareness, creativity, artistic and musical skills.

We can further state that the left hemisphere is primarily concerned with targeted, focused, detailed, single minded and black and white binary thinking.

The right hemisphere sees the big picture. It sees the world in terms of flow and interconnectedness. It sees uniqueness and context.

Therefore, we can say.

The left hemisphere helps us to work and live in the world.

The right hemisphere helps us to understand the world.

Our modern world with all its stresses and haste forces us to live using our cognitive right hemisphere brain. Our problem is that many of us do not recognize the existence of the left-brain hemisphere or, if we do, misunderstand its function. We think we are behaving rationally but we are not. The right brain exercises its control over our supposed rational cognitive thought behaviour, but we do not even acknowledge its existence. Therefore, how can we possibly be balanced?

It gets worse.

Continuing recklessness and rushing blindly onwards, without an awareness and understanding of this part of our brain, is having a detrimental impact on our species. We are not emotionally evolved enough as a species to cope with the pace at which our lives and technology now move, and the concept of only educating the cognitive function of the brain has the potential to bring an end to our species. How? If everything we do is left brain, focused, rational, narrow, and piecemeal then nothing can be balanced as the counterweight to this. Far seeing, contextualized interconnectedness is lost upon us. This binary selfish thinking has given rise to climate change, wars and famines, hyper loneliness and isolation, disconnectedness, and despair. This faulty way of thinking will cause both our personal undoing and the utter destruction of the world. Another way of putting all this is: our idea of knowledge, based solely upon cognition and brain function without understanding the deeper levels of consciousness and other ways of knowing, has caused us to develop disproportionally. We have become asymmetrical. We are proportionate to our wants, but disproportionate to our needs.

Human beings evolved to change and adapt slowly. In the past, this meant we had more than sufficient time to adapt and respond to our slowly changing environment. Therefore it is obvious that we cannot possibly cope with and adapt to the unprecedented rate of change, both in ourselves and the environment we currently face.

Our great difficulty is that because we have become accustomed to the modern concept of progress, we cannot conceive of anything else. Moving and evolving at such a great pace, as we indisputably now are, has a significant consequence. It becomes very difficult to see the ramifications of such rapid progress, and its effect on us as individuals, as a society, and as a planetary ecosystem. It is very difficult for us to see the system because we are in the system.

We know from science, physics and particularly from quantum

mechanics that everything that exists in a tangible way is just energy in one form or another. The physical world, the ecosystem we live in, and indeed all the things around us, including our very bodies, are made up of pure energy. The world itself is one giant, interconnected, harmonically balanced organism built on the very fundamental bricks of the universe, the quarks, and the other subatomic particles that make up everything that exists.

The world is an organism like a large single cell. It can only be healthy when it is in balance and in harmony. We as individuals can only be healthy when we are in balance and in harmony. Therefore, we can see that our interdependence and coexistence, as a species, as individuals, and fundamentally with the planet we live on, depends upon a harmonic and balanced system. This system, be it our body system, our ecosystem, our climate system, or any other form of system, is totally dependent on and rests upon the wellness and the understanding of the connectedness of all things. For us all to be well, and now for us to survive as a species, we must understand harmonic balance and its discordant equivalent.

Our goal is to live in harmony with all other living things and with our environment, of which we are the custodians. Therefore, if we fail in our guardianship, we will kill the very thing that sustains us. Unfortunately for us and for our planet, we are in a state of great imbalance. What is worse, it's a state of growing exponential imbalance, both in us as individuals and in the ecosystem in which we live.

It is indisputable that civilization and the planet are under enormous threat. The cause of this threat is us humans. In our precipitous rush towards perceived progress, we are fundamentally and terribly unaware of what we are doing. The direct consequence of this will be our imminent demise. Once again, because of our faulty, binary thinking, we have become ideologically embroiled in this catastrophe. Some of us refuse to accept it is a fact at all and some of us have become puritanically obsessed with the idea of climate change. We have our ideological perspectives. Meanwhile, the world gets warmer.

Perhaps if we framed it in a different way, it might help us to act instead of reacting in an ideological manner.

Instead of Climate Change, which is fraught with vested interests and controversy, let us call it an Environmental Crisis. We can see that something is wrong. This way we can deal with the symptoms at least until we may face reality.

We have history and form on this.

Many ancient and archaic civilizations failed because of rapid, unbalanced advancement that led to significant climate change. For example, the Indus valley civilization in modern day Pakistan and India and the Mayan civilization in Mesoamerica. Others can be added such as the ancient Accadian civilization in the middle east and Angkor Wat in Cambodia and many more. The significant difference is this: before, we humans always had somewhere else to go, some other part of the world to explore when we failed or caused catastrophic change. This time, because of the interconnectedness of the world and all who live on it, we have nowhere else to go. This is it. There is no New World.

It is apparent that our inability to deal with the current rapid rate of change, and our failure to establish a balanced, harmonious way of living with both ourselves and our environment, have led to an incipient climactic crisis. Our failure to act and to be aware of the damage we are doing to ourselves as individuals, to our society, and to our planet has obvious catastrophic consequences. However, we are not lost, because we can take responsibility and try to restore a harmonious balance. We can do this in an individual way and take responsibility for our own actions.

We must find a new way to live.

We humans have failed to adapt to the pace of our own evolution in the 21st century. Were we able to adapt our responses and behaviours to our changing circumstances and environment, then we would adapt very successfully. We did so for a very long time. We learned from our mistakes. We would be balanced as we were before, for countless millennia. However, when we struggle to adapt (which we are) our responses and behaviours become maladaptive and irrational.

It is technology that is evolving at pace now. We have outsourced so much of our cognitive brain to technology and, increasingly, to artificial intelligence, that our cognitive brain is being used less and less as we outsource more and more. Because we have not evolved emotionally as a species, we do not have the discernment to see the damage or the effects this 'Progress' and outsourcing are causing us.

The more we outsource and lose touch with our rational brain, the more we become open to manipulation. This is reducing all human experiences to qualities that can be diagnosed, tracked, graphed, and ultimately controlled. The journey that we see as progress is only taking us further and further away from awareness, and without awareness we will ultimately cease to exist.

Our physical planet is so sick now that it is on its last legs, but in many ways the ailing physical planet is just a mirror image of our ailing human species. The macrocosm is just a reflection of the microcosm. Our external world is in crisis, purely because our internal environment of self is in crisis.

The human society organism is grossly out of balance.

The world organism is grossly out of balance.

The individual organism is grossly out of balance.

Our symbiotic harmonious relationship with our planet has developed into a cancerous growth with fatal consequences.

We are not hopeless, however. We have shown many times before that we are resourceful beyond all imagining. If we would only take responsibility and act accordingly, then as a species we could restore balance to ourselves as individuals and as a society, and to the planet on which we live.

It is difficult for us to take responsibility without understanding what we must take responsibility for and how to go about it. This must be part of our dawning new awareness. Our quantum awareness.

The world is a very difficult place in which to live. It is rife with addiction, depression, unhappiness, war, and conflict. Suicide is increasing, just as is hopelessness and helplessness. We are increasingly battered and bewildered by all-pervasive social media messaging and the clear-cut breakdown of family and small society units. On top of this, disenfranchisement with government and the increasingly virulent spread of corporate consumer capitalism has led us to our worst disease of all. This is the disease of nihilism. The disease of despondency, despair, and hopelessness. This is the disease of societal suicide.

The only way we can counteract this is to become aware of it through information, leading to knowledge, understanding, and awareness. If we are not aware of something, we cannot do anything about it. We are not at fault and thus blame is inappropriate. It is our fault, however, if we have an inkling that something is not right with us or the world, and we fail to take responsibility for it and do something about it.

The more unbalanced everything becomes, the greater our lack of awareness. To really become well and flourish as a species, we need to become aware. Awareness is not an easy thing as it often means having to face our fears, truths, and failings as humans on the planet. However, though this may be difficult to achieve in the short term, it will be hugely rewarding in the long term.

The need for us all to become aware and see the need to change the way that we do things is obvious. We need to look closely and be honest. Fundamentally we need to be able to recognize the truth when we see it. We need to get into reality. Change is a very difficult thing to achieve. It means looking at ourselves in a new way, critically but with compassion. Most of us spend a lifetime waiting for other people and things to change and do not realize that we can change ourselves. In order to change something, we first must know what it is we are trying to change. Achieving that requires understanding and a broader view of self and the world.

Change is difficult as it means having to come into reality, which can be very painful place to be in the short term. I know this because I have spent a great deal of my life living in unreality, in the hell of addiction, depression, anxiety, and coercive control, and using denial and pretense as my default position.

Having come through a protracted period of pain and suffering, I realized that meaning and truth could be found, and that it was their absence that caused the malaise in the first place. In the early stages of recovery, reality was a very difficult place for me to be, but I also learned that if I did not become aware and face up to my own reality, I would die.

When I began to face my reality and find love and compassion for myself, I was also able to find reality in and compassion for others in a real and truthful way. Only then was I able to create a space that allowed me to go back and create awareness and reconciliation around my life story. It was by doing this consistently over time that I truly learned that reality was the only way to experience the world in a truly meaningful way, first for myself and subsequently for society. How do you find your way to reality? Here is what I discovered that changed my life and can change the life of anybody willing to participate in the 'Way' outlined in this book.

This is my story, and the resultant programme I created for wellness.

CHAPTER 1

MY STORY

My name is Paddy Rafter. I am a singer, musician, poet, painter, former college lecturer in engineering physics, academy director, racehorse trainer, farmer, husband, father, brother, grandfather, and friend. I have lived a very difficult but also a very blessed life. I have lived a life of addiction and trauma from a very young age. This has led me to some very dark places in which I have damaged myself and have also damaged and hurt the lives of all those close to me.

Therefore, I realized that I was Paddy Rafter: a drunk, an addict, an unreliable and self-centered person. I was a failure ridden with shame and guilt. I was beyond redemption and hope, cast from the world. I was invalid.

On my journey of return I discovered that I was none of the negative descriptors listed above. The day I discovered that I was me was the day I started to become well. Everything else was just an attachment.

This is also a story of trauma that started at a very early age. In order that you can initially identify with my story, I will lay out the bare facts in this chapter. This is, therefore, the story of how it was, what happened, and what arose from this series of events.

I had an idyllic early childhood, but in my early teens I was sent to live in the countryside with my grandparents. I had periodically lived with my grandparents since I was about seven or eight, but then went to live with them permanently, which I found very lonely and very difficult. I felt a great sense of abandonment and became very traumatized and insecure. I was not liked or accepted in my grandparents' house, and most of my relatives really disliked me because of who I was. I was the boy who would someday inherit the farm.

Added to this was the fact that I struggled with school and found it very difficult. I never felt accepted, even though I had been very good both academically and at sport until I reached secondary (high) school. I experienced a lot of beatings from teachers, and a lot of bullying from fellow students, until I learned to fight back. I had to walk eight miles a day to school and was constantly laughed at and ridiculed because of my ill-fitting dirty clothes and poor hygiene. This contributed to an increasingly poor attendance record.

I had my first nervous breakdown at the age of ten. This was the culmination of being made to stand by the classroom wall (a form of punishment) for three months, all day every day, and I subsequently collapsed in the schoolyard. Consequently, I did not attend school for the next six months, and I became very unwell. During that period, the family doctor would attend to me in my home two or three times a week. Also, during this period, my parents arranged for the local priest to come and visit me twice a week.

As I began to feel a little bit better in myself, I started to visit the local church each day, a hundred yards away from my home, and pray. This eventually led to me sitting and praying in the church for hours on end, all day every day, becoming increasingly distressed.

The more I prayed, the more my sense of disbelief increased. I became more and more confused, then distraught and quite unable to distinguish between dreams and reality. My sense of futility and failure was enormous. Failure at being unable to believe, and futility because I could see no sense or meaning beyond belief. I envied the priests and other people their certainty, and I felt I was forgotten, even by God.

Eventually I was consigned to bed again. I did not sleep for almost three months, and from then on, I lived in fear, all day every day. This period was also a very difficult one for my parents. They endured the loss of three children who were born and died in infancy. That loss was ameliorated in some small way for them, with the birth of a healthy baby daughter. This allowed them to move on somewhat, and I was sent back on a permanent basis to my grandparents' house in the country. This was to be my home until I went away to college.

The unintended consequence of this was that I was placed in a very hostile environment where I felt totally alone, abandoned, and rejected. This was not my parent's fault, they were just unaware of what was happening. I now see that my parents were deeply traumatized as they had to leave the family farm three weeks after they got married and they never really got over this fact. This was why they were so attached to the farm they had lost in the first place. Another unintended consequence was that my constant companions were fear and hunger. Living with them was my reality for a long time. All of my teenage years were very troubled and traumatic. I loved music and singing but when I tried to do guitar lessons my schoolteacher, who was a Christian brother, found out and beat me up and called me a little girl. I had no sense of self-worth or value, and this was the way I continued to feel about myself. I spent most of my time in my teenage years working with horses. I worked with them on the farm. I worked with horses by hiring myself and my horse out to neighboring farmers to make some money. When I was on time off, I would ride to the most inaccessible places I could find. This was the only time that I felt safe. Horses became the only individuals that I could trust. Horses were my refuge in loneliness and despair. I formed a bond with horses that has never left me.

When I went away to college, suddenly a whole new vista opened up and I could do a lot of the things I could not do before. However, the trauma and pain came with me, and initially I found it very difficult to integrate with people. I worked part time for a construction firm to pay my fees and to live. I was really struggling, financially and emotionally. Then came the fateful day when I first really engaged with alcohol. What a difference it made immediately. Soon I was on top of the world. I was doing great in college, doing a second degree and then a third. I was confident. I was popular. I was at every party. I was singing with bands and doing music in college as well, there were girls and they wanted to be with me. There was everything I thought I ever wanted and so much more. This was a life beyond my wildest dreams. I had discovered that good self-medication with alcohol really helped, for two very different reasons. It helped me to feel so much more confident in myself, and at the same time it took away the pain, the suffering, and the trauma, for a little while at least. It worked like a wonder drug.

It was a wonder drug.

For a little while, a few years, everything was simply wonderful. I did fantastic in college, played in bands, studied music, and went out having fun every night of the week. Alcohol was my constant companion and it never let me down.

I got married at a young age, after completing college. At the same time, I was studying music with a realistic prospect of becoming a very successful international operatic tenor.

Unfortunately, instead of making progress I regressed. The pain and the trauma had not gone away but had merely hidden. Having a wife and young children (and thus more responsibilities) at home, as well as an increasingly demanding professional career, I found myself unable to deal with the reality of my situation. I resorted more and more to alcohol to prop up my false sense of self and my illusions. Instead, I became progressively more unwell and more deluded. Because of my inability to cope, and because I was increasingly unable to think for myself, I became consumed by and totally under the control of alcohol. This led me to hurt myself and everybody that was close and important to me.

Addiction led me to do terrible things, stupid things, and eventually took everything I had away from me. I did not achieve anything like the heights I was capable of, nor could I maintain close, loving relationships in a real and meaningful way. Instead, I hurt everybody close to me; unintentionally and unaware, I sprinkled hurt the way others sprinkle confetti at a wedding. I became even more unstable and even more addicted, and I was powerless to do anything about it.

I had my first incarceration in a mental hospital at this point. It was one of very many incarcerations I was to have in mental hospitals, but they really didn't work for me. If anything, I became more traumatized and stigmatized. The one positive thing that came from all this was the patients I met. Some were mad, some were sad, some were bad, and some were broken, but they were all real and devoid of conceit or arrogance.

Some of the kindest people I ever met were patients in those hospitals. No matter how I tried, I couldn't stop and I couldn't change. I was in the midst of a cycle of unrelenting and repetitive misery. In terrible pain, suffering and hopeless, with suicidal thoughts a constant companion, all that ever worked for me was to medicate myself out of it, to go into fantasy. I needed to get away from the world which I found impossible to live in.

Eventually I found a way to stop, through a rigorous course of action and self-control. I did this through a mixture of Alcoholics Anonymous (AA), counselling, and AA friends, but ultimately through white-knuckled abstinence and diversion into other things.

I spent the following twenty years singing, both in opera and in concert, painting, and working as a racehorse trainer. I also became a successful college lecturer. I was a husband and father as best I could be, and I really tried my best. I was everything and nothing. I was not capable of fully immersing myself in any of these facets of my life, because I could not give myself to anything in a full way. I spent my time diverting my attention from myself and struggling to keep my addiction at bay. More than anything, I wanted my children to have a good life and to have better education and opportunities than I had. I always thought I could do much better. It was not my fault even though I thought that it was, so I blamed myself consistently throughout this period. I had a great sense of guilt, recrimination, shame, and self-sabotage. This eventually led me back to addiction, which was much worse the second time around.

Once again I hurt everybody around me, my wife, my children, my friends, and I almost lost everything, including my life. I spent years in hell, each day worse than the day before. In the midst of this, when I was in intensive care in hospital, I told myself that there must be another way, that I could not go on like this anymore. I could either die or find another way to live.

I have since devoted all my time to trying to learn to live a better life, to have a life that befits a human being. To repair the damage I have caused to others, to repair the damage that I have caused to myself. In the mix of all of this I have discovered a way to live, a way to be that allows me and us all to be free and happy.

The whole purpose of this book and the 48 Acts it contains is to help all to live life in peace and harmony, free from addictions. It is also to help you cope in this increasingly frenetic and meaningless world. Through the suffering and pain, I have endured, I have learned much. I have learned to die to my old life, in order to live a new life. If I can help you by collating and disseminating these new ideas in this form, then it will all have been worth it.

This book is relevant and has meaning to just about anybody in society. As can be seen from the previous chapter, our society is struggling in a way it has never struggled before. We as individuals are struggling in a way we have never done before.

We are all on a continuum. There are many of us who do not identify as being unhappy or addicted. They cope with life perfectly fine on their own terms. On the other hand, there are those of us on this continuum whose lives are greatly impacted by addiction, anxiety, obesity, depression, and coercive controlling relationships. On the same continuum there are people who feel left out, who cannot understand why they are so unhappy, even though they appear to have everything.

If you feel you are in a rut, if you feel like a failure, if you feel disappointed that you have not achieved your potential, or if life has been unkind to you, you are not alone. If you feel that you are not who you wanted to be, or if you feel unloved or unloving, dissatisfied, and cynical, then this book is for you. But this is for all of us, this book, and the ideas it contains. We are all there somewhere. We are all lost here somewhere.

These acts will lead you to a new path, a new road to freedom. I know this book will help you, as it is based on absolute truth and reality. I never knew what truth and reality were, and it was only when I arrived there that I discovered freedom and wellness.

If you give yourself to these Acts, you will learn a way that will allow you to have unimaginable peace of mind and happiness in your life. This new learning will show you that you really can achieve those things that you missed out on or were beyond you for whatever reason.

The basic purpose of these 48 Acts is to give you information, which leads to knowledge, which leads to understanding, which leads to awareness.

CHAPTER 2

THE POWER OF THE DRUGS OF APPROVAL AND APPRECIATION

On my own lifelong journey of understanding my own unhappiness and addictions, I realized that long before I discovered alcohol and all my maladaptive behaviours were made manifest, I had first become addicted to the power of the drugs of approval and appreciation. This happened when I was an infant and child. Indeed, this happens to all of us. It is normal, it is part of our development within our family and society. We all need to feel that we belong. This is profoundly so in childhood. This whole process is the conditioning that will never leave us, no matter how old we get or whatever our circumstances.

We all need to feel appreciation and approval. When, for whatever reason, we do not feel approval, we will go to any extreme to find it, and the worst thing is that we are not quite sure what "it" actually is.

The most important thing for our future, for our continuity as a species, is our children. The future of our society obviously depends on well-adjusted, authentic children who grow up to be compassionate, kind, and aware adults. We as a society and species are failing drastically. Why are we failing so catastrophically now? There is general agreement, right across the world, that our world system is in jeopardy. The richest countries in the world are in chaos. The poorest countries in the world are in chaos. The only difference is the cause of the problems. The impact of rich countries on poor countries is very significant. We all share the planet and, whether we like it or not, the threat of nuclear war, the environmental crisis, the disparity of wealth, the advent of A.I. affect us all profoundly.

The biggest crisis facing us humans however is the crisis of 'Disbelief'.

Nobody believes anybody. Everything is fake. The specter of unbelief and distrust shadows the whole world. Why is this so?

We cannot cope with the rate of change in our society and in the world. This is further exacerbated by the models of governments and commerce we choose or have chosen for us. Unfortunately, and I really mean unfortunately, our commercial *modus operandi* has become corrupt, parasitic, and deadly. The capitalist consumer culture which has been created by and for us is the logical outcome of our societal evolution. This free market consumer culture has many conveniences and benefits for us. This culture has evolved in tandem with us. Increased industrialization and population move-ment from the land to cities in the last two hundred and fifty years has come with increased anxiety and stress.

The inevitable consequences of the free market economy, if left unchecked, are that it grows exponentially and becomes more dereg-ulated and more dehumanized. We are making a grave mistake. We are not understanding our growth and development. We are failing to see the consequences of our actions. In this free-market consumer culture, people and society at large do not matter to those in power. People are just consumers or end users, and there is no altruism inherent in commercialism. They are obviously mutually incompati-ble. We are seduced by marketing; because of the extreme rapidity of the development of technology, the capitalist consumer culture doctrine is disseminated pervasively and permanently. The conse-quences of our abrogation of responsibility and our failure to see and understand what is really happening in the world are stark, possibly causing the end of our species.

If we do not have adaptive, responsive children, who can cope with whatever circumstances are presented to them, we are surely lost.

The children of today experience many traumas in their early years which would not have happened years ago. From as early as they can hold a screen or tablet, they can be instantly exposed to violence and sex at the touch of a button, all with no context, and long before their brains are developed enough to process what they are seeing or experiencing. Although there were traumas years ago, they were obvious and equitable. You either lived or you died. You either survived or you did not. It was normal and normative. Now we have complex trauma. It is all of our fault, and it is none of our fault.

Right from our birth we are taught by our parents, caregivers, and early schoolteachers the use of, and the power of the drug of approval. When we act in accordance with their wishes, we are approved and appreciated. When we act contrary to their wishes, we experience disapproval and misappreciation. This is a key understanding. When you understand this, you understand how approval is so beneficial for us humans. You also begin to understand why it is so seductive and addictive.

You can also understand how easily some people can manipulate this key knowledge for their own ends. This is how control and destruction are so easily wielded and so pervasive.

This early experience of reward and recrimination are subsequently mirrored in a myriad of other addictions and maladaptive behaviors.

You will also now see that this is how so many of us become addicted. We become addicted to power, money, control, and sex.

We become addicted to alcohol, drugs, and substance abuse in general.

We become addicted to maladaptive behaviours.

We are addicted to the drugs of approval and appreciation.

We are all addicts on the spectrum.

We as addicts then become easily manipulated.

From their earliest age, humans seek approval. We all do. It is in our nature to do so. The extraordinarily dangerous new development is that our children are becoming more and more easily manipulated from a younger age by external controlling forces. They are manipulated through social media and everywhere that consumer culture can reach them. They are being manipulated, and because they have become more easily accessible through social media, they are being made into addicts.

I genuinely believe that there is an exponential increase of uneasiness and anxiety in society, and we do not have the awareness, understanding, or tools to deal with this state of unease. So, we compensate by looking constantly for approval just about everywhere or anywhere. We are confused.

Just like a child, or any animal with its mother, we are seeking approval and reassurance. We are getting the wrong reassurance from the wrong people. Our big problem is that we do not recognize this. So, when you feel good through this constant "false" approval, it becomes a part of your authenticity and identity. This is a false concept or belief. Therefore, your identity and authenticity are compromised.

This need for constant approval ('Aren't I good' and 'Please like me') is ubiquitous. Thus, there is an out-of-balance desire to look for approval and feel appreciated. It is the exact same thing as the cravings of the most desperate and unfortunate drug addict looking for a drug that he or she can't get.

It is becoming more and more difficult for children to grow up into finely balanced, integrated members of society now, as everything is so out of balance at all ages, but especially among our younger people who are more vulnerable to this type of manipulation. This is because it has become the accepted norm that more and more time is spent online and on social media, and less time is spent integrating among friends in the real world.

A child six, seven, or eight years of age is on social media where everything is addictive approval. This reinforces something that the child has learned before they can verbalize it: approval. 'How many likes did I get?' It becomes like a drug. This need for approval is an addiction.

We as humans have always sought approval, and with the advent of social media it is becoming much more virulent, topical, and constant. It is everywhere, this need. People feel the overwhelming need to belong to virtual groups, to have people say nice things about them. They are constantly seeking approval, doctoring photos, and creating a false lifestyle.

This is not even really you, all this craving for a drug of approval. But what you are really doing is creating an inauthentic version of yourself, and I know, through my own addictions and struggles, the consequences of being the 'unauthenticated you' later on in your life.

As this type of young person, or indeed any person, gets older, they become more and more desperate, more and more unhappy. They have no idea why they are so unhappy because all they know is the constant search for approval, to be wanted in a specific way.

It is inevitable that we will end up with a whole society totally addicted to approval, and the consequences of this are catastrophic. Everything becomes an externalized version of you. This is the creation of the 'False Self' or the 'Ego'.

Thus, everything about you becomes false, shallow, seeking approval, and addicted to drugs you don't even realize are controlling you. You seek approval for where you live, what you wear, what you eat, how you look, who your friends are, and are constantly getting other people to make your decisions and choices for you.

I was recently talking to a person who had just gotten married. In the course of the conversation, I asked her if she had enjoyed her wedding day. She told me that she could not tell me until she had a proper look at the wedding video. I thought that this was so sad, as the only way she could authenticate her feelings was by making sure that everything had been perfect aesthetically; her measuring stick for a lovely wedding was based on everybody else's approval. In effect, she was a nonparticipant at her own wedding.

The logical consequence of all this is a validation that says 'I am unlovable. I am rejectable.' Thus, the validation becomes an invalidation. This is because you believe that unless you measure up to and adhere to these rigorous strictures and structures being placed upon you, then you and your life are a failure. You are invalid unless and until you receive validation from an external source. You need your drug.

These are faulty belief systems. You have received faulty programming from very early in life. You are surrounded by and bombarded by images of your failure, so unless you are well-integrated and balanced, this is going to affect you.

Most people do not know how to self-validate or to come into awareness in any form, so they draw erroneous conclusions based on the information that they have. People will go to any lengths to get approval, especially on digital platforms. They then start to make unhealthy choices as conformity and a certain lifestyle become almost obligatory.

This is what all addictions do; they get out of control, so you need the supply more and more. All this occurs despite the negative and accumulating consequences. Your need for your drug or supply will override all logical and practical rationale. This exact same behaviour can be applied to families, communities and even states. Slowly, we become that which we most abhor.

Furthermore, if we define how a species is doing by the success of its offspring, and the prognosis for its future, then we must surely define our progress as increasingly concerning. There is no other way you could look at this and say anything else could be true. This generation is leaving many consequences of our actions on the generations that will follow. It really is as the bible says, 'The sins of the father will be visited on the sons to the seventh generation'. The modern meaning is; Due to the greed, stupidity and lack of awareness of our generation, the generations that will follow will pay a heavy price in every facet of their lives.

Now we are living in a world where there is no verification of the truth, where nobody has enough money, where communities are becoming virtual communities. It is a fear-driven world, everybody feels isolated, and addictions are becoming more and more common because of the way we have evolved, especially in the past couple of hundred years. We have evolved in a way that is so out of balance with that which is around us, that we are on a mission to destruction.

Everybody has bought into this, but it is primarily promoted by legacy media, consumerism, capitalist culture, throwaway culture, social media, and the need for judging and scapegoating people. The only way that we can fix these things and be released from their chains of bondage is to become aware of what is happening, and then set in place real structures that will revalidate the nature and value of people in a more holistic way. In order to do that, we need to totally reevaluate human needs, as distinct from their wants.

It will be a huge challenge to break this cycle of addiction to approval and appreciation, and to get people to see that it has the same effect on the mind as an addiction to drugs, alcohol, gambling, or sex. As people become increasingly entrenched in this addiction, unfortunately, they become less and less able to see it.

The only way breaking the cycle can be done is through awareness. Becoming aware of what is going on, and then putting things in place to deal with them. The key is awareness and being able to name the problems.

This pseudo life of digital social media, coupled with our innate need for approval and appreciation, will lead to an untrammeled catastrophe. This catastrophe will be the breakdown of our society.

CHAPTER 3
THE DAWNING OF AWARENESS

The dawning of awareness for me was that moment when I knew I was going to die. I wanted to die because the pain was so bad. Yet, deep down, there was a part of me that wanted to live, that almost felt obliged to reach my potential that I knew I was capable of achieving. I just did not know how.

The beginning of this programme of awareness was to try to learn to live in truth and reality, no matter how painful this reality was. I had to learn what the truth really was. I had no idea what truth was, as I had concocted a world of unreality purely to survive the hell I constantly lived in.

I began to seek and look for knowledge, knowledge about me. Why had I arrived where I was? This was my starting point for the accumulation of knowledge. I had no idea that my constant seeking of approval and appreciation as a child, purely to survive those awful deep-rooted feelings of abandonment, rejection, isolation, and loneliness, had created my faulty programming and skewed my belief systems. These in turn completely messed up my view of the world, and of myself.

My false beliefs had led me into a world of addiction, depression, anxiety, and the forming of deeply coercive, controlling relationships.

I sought knowledge of all these afflictions just as a starting point to help me understand myself in a different way. I discovered that if I was able to write about these afflictions, and see them for what they really were, then I could create awareness about them and begin the journey of change.

This is the essence of what I learned, and if you can see yourself in this, know that you can change, because I did.

Therefore, you can infer that one of the first things you have to learn is the willingness and ability to see things in a new way. To see with a 'Big Seeing'. What is the meaning of the term; Big Seeing'? To learn to see the whole picture with all of the facts or knowledge we possess in a dispassionate way devoid of our ideology or conditioning. To see the whole, not the part. To see the interconnectedness of all things.

ADDICTION

You know why you are here. I can help.

Addiction is best defined as:

Craving an addictive substance or behaviour to experience temporary pleasure or relief from pain and being unable to give it up despite increasing negative consequences.

Addiction is a way to escape reality.

Addiction is a response to trauma.

However, we who have experienced addiction in its awful reality know that it is much more than this.

I have spent a lifetime in addiction and in trying to understand it. I would define it as follows:

Addiction is hell on earth; it takes your pride and self-respect and leaves you with nothing. It takes your voice. It is the craving that you can never satisfy.

Addiction causes you to hurt everybody around you and destroy their lives. It will hurt and damage your spouse/partner and children if you have any. It will cause you to destroy your family. Then it takes all your friends, your money, your dignity, your voice, your health— and that is only the beginning.

Eventually you will hurt everybody around you so much that they will have nothing to do with you, and still, you will continue.

You may end up in hospital, in jail, or in a mental institution, and all you will think about is your addiction. If the addiction is to a substance, you will only think about how you can get it as quickly as possible.

You will think you are right and everybody else is wrong. You will build an empire of hurt, and ultimately every road in addiction leads to devastation. Having destroyed the life of your spouse, children, mother, father, brothers, sisters, and friends, you will still continue on your own. You cannot stop. The only way out is death.

Your mind is not your own, and here I will separate addiction into two different parts.

If your addiction is primarily behavioral, then you will end up shattered and devastated, cast out, unwanted, untouchable. Your name will be destroyed, your character destroyed, and you will be less than the least of all things.

If your addiction is to a substance or substances, then you will be all of the above and more. You will crave the substance more, but it will do less and less for you. You need more of your drug and para-doxically, it gives you less and less relief.

You will lie. You will steal. You will cheat until you do not know who you are. You will despise the self you already hate. Then addiction will take your mind and your soul, and if you are lucky, you will go mad.

Addiction affects your mind, your body, your health, and your soul because it is a soul sickness. Your self-hate will know no bounds.

You will become that which you most despise: your addicted self.

You do not have to live like this.

Why do you do this?

The reasons are manifold and complex. People will give you simplistic reasons, but there are none. You do this because you are completely unaware of both yourself and the world you live in. You are not in reality.

Why?

You do this as a response to the pain that you experience every day. This pain may stem from childhood or adolescence. It may come from your experiences as a child and what you saw or perceived in the world. It may come from what you experienced as an adolescent. It also may come from what you experienced as an adult.

Fundamentally, addiction in its full-blown sense is an inability to cope with the world and the pain you experience.

Active addiction.

- It is fundamentally a way to cope.
- It is fundamentally a way to escape reality.
- It is fundamentally a way to survive.
- It is fundamentally a way to escape pain.
- It is ultimately a way to escape you.

As addiction progresses and becomes exponentially worse, affecting your life or work or family, you will have many different experiences of trying to stop your descent into darkness and madness.

Your friends, your workplace, and your family especially, will try to help you; your family will be the last to let you go. You will have numerous violations of the law, and escapades with law enforcement in some cases. You will be encouraged and, in some cases, forced to go into treatment centers.

Most of these treatment centers will try to help you. But because they fundamentally do not understand the power of addiction and its real causes, more often than not they will be ineffective and in many cases do more harm than good (as was my own personal experience). Addiction treatment centers do indeed admit that their success rate is less than three per cent.

Following the Minnesota model, as most do, they will deconstruct you mercilessly in the mistaken belief that you are unaware of how bad things are. They will reinforce in you the idea that you are an invalid member of society at large. They will also tell you how reprehensible you are, both to yourself and those close to you.

The sad consequence of this 'treatment' is that the remains of any of your self-respect will be destroyed. Regrettably, they then send you back out into the world without anything except a heightened sense of self-hate.

Others will use religious and secular cures, all well-meaning of course. The mental health services in your country will, initially at least, use cognitive behavioral therapy. These are really just short-term crisis intervention solutions, and offer no long-term, sustainable pathway forward for your addiction treatment.

Gurus and self-proclaimed experts in books and on media will try to help in their way with advice about self-forgiveness and self-love. And though this might be effective for a very small minority, for the vast majority this is almost impossible, as this is a love we have never experienced and of which we know nothing.

We live in shame. Shame of ourselves and shame of who we have become. Shame of the hurt we have caused others. Eventually everybody will give up on us and we will be on the streets, and nobody will want to know. It really is an impossible situation. We have become so deceitful that we cannot be trusted. We know this of course but we will do anything to get our drug, our supply.

Why me?

'Why me?'

Did you deserve this? No, of course you did not. This is a fate worse than death. This is the prolonged death dance, and you are a helpless participant caught between the music and the dance.

Can I get well?

'How can I get well?'

You can get out any time you wish, and you do not need to descend in chains into the depths of hell. Not all of us must reach the bottom. I like the analogy of a building lift or elevator. You can get out at any level you like If you follow the programme I am suggesting to you. Then you have a very good chance to live a happy, healthy, and contented life.

You can rebuild your life and gain back your self-respect. You can break free from all the chains of hate and hurt.

How?

You need to understand.

You need to become aware.

You need to put work in. There is no knight in shining armor riding to save you.

The Reward

You can be free. You can get your voice back.

It will not be easy, but nothing valuable ever is. You can have a life beyond your wildest dreams and live in peace and contentment with yourself. You can reconcile and come to terms with the things you have done in the past that have caused you to hold on to so much shame, guilt, hurt, regret, and darkness. You can look to a brighter, happier future.

I have been in all these dark places.

I have been in treatment centers.

I have been locked up in mental institutions. I have been homeless.

I have hurt my wife and my children immeasurably. I have hurt my friends.

I have destroyed everything good around me.

I have lost everything. I have hurt myself.

I have been in hell.

But I got well, and if I got well then you can too.

We have just seen that our response to the childhood drugs of approval and appreciation, and our childhood programming, may often result in substance abuse or misuse, leading us to devastating consequences.

In the exact same way and for the exact same reasons, we may instead resort to maladaptive behavioral responses to our childhood drugs and programming.

These responses are just as devastating and even more pervasive in society. We resort to unreality by our behaviour. Again, our response is the same. We can't cope with reality and our perceived failures to measure up to the expectations of others. Thus, because we can't understand the world as it is, we leave the world in various different ways and stages into a perceived reality which is totally at variance with the real reality. In each case, we can see that it is our perception of reality that is the problem.

In some cases, we may have very strong and traumatic events in our childhood and adolescence which confirm our programming. This reinforcement of trauma is critical, because unless we can get into reality as opposed to 'perceived reality', it will always lead us to maladaptive behaviours in one form or another. Unfortunately, though these maladaptive behaviours are not our fault, we bear the brunt and the consequences.

It behooves us, therefore, to isolate and identify other significant maladaptive behaviours which are running rampant in our world today and are having devastating consequences on individuals and society at large. We will describe them, what they are, where they come from, their consequences, and the real failure to deal with them in any long-term, significant way by the established treatment constructs.

There is, at present, no long-term pathway to treating anxiety, depression, or other chronic maladaptive behaviours. The reason for this is that these problems and maladaptive behaviours are endemic in our society. So much so, that we are only creating short-term crisis intervention solutions, which are not sustainable in the long term. In other words, we medicate depression and anxiety. You can immediately see the problem with this medication therapy. We are replacing one drug or behaviour with another. Indeed the only difference is that the medication is a prescription drug instead of an illicit one.

I truly believe that if you follow the 48 Acts, then your life can be transformed, and these afflictions will never trouble you again.

I am firmly convinced that the 48 Acts and all that they contain offer a way of living for everybody, no matter your situation, religion, orientation, or belief system. They offer a way to live well in this chaotic world, with peace, harmony, and stability of mind. I'm further convinced that they should be in every classroom, every village and community, every town and city and, indeed, in every international forum. Close adherence to the principles contained within these Acts will undoubtedly change us as individuals and society as a whole.

Anxiety

What is meant by Anxiety?

Anxiety is an instinctive reaction to the body's natural fear response for survival. Everybody has feelings of anxiety at some point in their life, whether it is about preparing for a job interview, their first day in school, an exam, or meeting their partner's parents for the first time. We associate anxiety with alterations to our mental state, experienced as worry or apprehension perhaps, and physical symptoms such as raised heart rate and adrenaline.

We also understand that it is likely to affect us only until the source of our anxiety has passed, or until we have learned to cope with it.

Anxiety, therefore, is one of a range of emotions that serves the positive function of alerting us to things we might need to take care of: things that are potentially harmful.

More importantly, these emotions help us to evaluate potential threats and respond to them in an appropriate way, perhaps by quickening our reflexes or focusing our attention.

Anxiety is an emotional state that can work for us as well as against us. It is something we all have in common, but where we differ is in how we perceive these feelings of arousal and how we respond to them. Our life circumstances, our upbringing, and our programming can all be factors in how we respond to anxiety.

What Happens when Anxiety Takes Over?

Where anxiety is concerned, everybody is on a continuum. On the lower end, we may have or feel no anxiety at all. That would not be good for us as we all need a certain amount of anxiety to get the job done. We would be catatonic or totally indifferent to the outcome of whatever may happen. This would lead to a poor outcome for us. However, if we have too much anxiety, we can end up on the higher end of the continuum and develop an anxiety disorder. This outcome is equally poor for us,

When anxiety takes over, it takes over your whole life. Usually, it starts in small incremental stages, and when we leave it unchecked or unexamined it grows rapidly. Eventually this leads to devastating consequences for our lives.

Basically, when anxiety starts to become a serious problem, fear takes over. As I said, all fear has its place, in limited circumstances and scope. However, when fear becomes all-pervasive it makes our lives unmanageable, and all the fun and enjoyment is gone. The beauty and thrill of life is replaced by fears: fear of the unknown, unnamed fears, dread, and terror. Anxiety also manifests itself in us in physical ways. If we don't learn to understand anxiety and deal with it in a real and proper way, we will never achieve any of the things that we wish to achieve, or we will fail to continue with those which we have begun. We will fail to have proper relationships or set proper boundaries, and we will have a very skewed perception of the world and reality around us.

Anxiety is a maladaptive behaviour that is used to deal with reality.

Anxiety is a response to trauma.

Anxiety is an inability to cope with the reality of the world as our perceptions are misconceived at best, or deeply flawed at worst.

Thus, we can see that it is a response to our programming and, indeed, to our drugs of approval and appreciation. We feel we can never measure up to the expectations of others, or our own expectations.

We feel we will never be good enough, clever enough, attractive enough, and all the other similar things associated with the judgement of others. Thus, we become anxious, more and more, bit by bit.

We hear and experience the world through the colored lens of a media deliberately trying to create danger and catastrophe in order to sell their products. Everywhere we are confronted with fear, be it individual or society based.

Climate crisis, food and power shortages, war after war. The message is always the same—imminent danger! Fight! Flight! Freeze! —all day every day.

We can see that because of our programming and our evolution over millions and millions of years, we are triggered to respond to the threat of danger immediately, from when we were primates and even long before. However, the stress went away quickly as we either fought the tiger or ran away from the tiger, and we learned to associate sounds, sights, and places with the tiger and avoid them in future.

Unfortunately for us, our brain is unable to distinguish the difference between reality and the perception of reality, just as we have seen.

Therefore, if the messaging that we are receiving twenty-four hours a day, seven days a week, is fear and fear-based, then we are obviously going to respond in an anxious way, because anxiety is just a natural response or behaviour that has become maladaptive. Fear has taken over.

I know this from my own experience, the feeling of fear and the overwhelming, constant, underlying anticipation of waiting for something dreadful to happen. It almost never does happen; but it's not the happening that's the problem, it's the anticipation of a perceived reality that it will.

I grew up with a pervasive sense of dread. In my case, I eventually had to medicate to get away from my fears.

People suffering from anxiety are given prescription medications of ever-increasing potency. They feel compelled to take them to get away from their fears, but as you can see the outcome is the same: an ever-increasing sense of hopelessness, despondency, and despair. A fundamental lack of self-authenticity. There is absolutely nothing wrong with having to take medications to allay the worst effects of an anxiety episode. Nor should we be in any way ashamed of doing so, or of going to seek medical help in this particular case. It will buy us time. But we must use this time to work through this programme and establish the real reasons for our anxiety in the first place. The huge danger for us is that we become trapped in the symptomatic treatment instead of addressing the underlying cause. When we begin to identify the underlying cause, then we may begin to deal with it effectively.

When I played sports, and especially when I performed on stages all over the world, I became increasingly proficient at my craft. Yet, rather than feeling a lessening of anxiety, I felt an increase of it as my perceived understanding of the expectations of the audience diverged from the reality of what it was. Over time my anxiety increased exponentially to the point where it became crippling, and I was unable to perform.

Fundamentally this programme is about a new way of looking at and a new way of seeing the world. Only then can you be present in the world. Only then will you have Agency.

Part of the reason I created the 48 Acts was that, through suffering and the subsequent journey of understanding, I learnt how to manage my anxiety. It plays no negative part in my life now. I learned to live and act. I learned to be present.

I did it using the precepts set out in these 48 Acts. If you do the same and follow the programme assiduously, then it will surely work for you and set you free from this crippling affliction, the maladaptive behaviour that is anxiety.

If you follow the programme set out in this book, you will get an unfamiliar and original perspective on a new way of living. Understanding why you have become the way you are will help to lower your anxieties.

You will have **information, knowledge, understanding, and awareness.** You will be free.

Accepting this situation, you will have the confidence to move on and live life.

If I have gotten well then you can also.

Depression

What do we mean by Depression?

You feel miserable and bad about yourself most of the time and are increasingly preoccupied with negative ideas about your life and the world. You do not feel motivated about most of the things you used to enjoy or were good at. You find everything an effort. You sleep poorly. If this is you, then it is likely you have a form of depression.

Different types of depression exist, with symptoms ranging from low mood to severe or catatonic inertia. Generally, depression does not result from a single event, but from a mix of events and factors.

Depression is on a continuum with good mental health conditions on the lower end and severe mental health effects on the high end. It is not life events that make us depressed; it is how we perceive and respond to these events that makes us unwell. Depression doesn't happen overnight; you do not wake up depressed one morning. Your slide into depression is incremental, and without awareness you suddenly arrive there without any trace or knowledge of how you got there.

Depression affects how you think, how you feel, and how you behave and exist in the world.

Feelings Caused by Depression:

Sadness, misery, oppression, irritability, feeling overwhelmed, guilt, frustration, lack of confidence, indecisiveness, and inability to concentrate.

You may already be medically diagnosed with depression. You may be on medication. There is no shame or guilt associated with taking medication, and it may indeed be the case that you might have to remain on medication for a long time. However, the 48 Acts will significantly alleviate your feelings and their causes. Your medication is constant and is necessary. You can work this programme in association with any medication you are on. You may find in time that you are able to lessen your dosage, or even end it, as the case may be. It is not significant.

The bad feelings of depression usually start gradually. You slowly become aware that you are feeling miserable and unhappy most of the time. It gets broader and deeper.

You become indecisive, you are unable to concentrate and keep your mind on anything—even reading or any other form of satisfaction and relaxation.

As you move further along the continuum, you feel as if you are looking at the world through fog and find yourself strangely untouched by the bad or sad things that happen to others. You can be disappointed with yourself, and feel irritable, frustrated, and angry with yourself and others. You feel powerless to fight against it. At night, you can't get to sleep because of the worries going round and round in your head, or you wake early, and you can't get back to sleep. Or maybe you find yourself sleeping all day—a thick, unrefreshing sleep which is just a means of not being awake, a means of shutting out the suffering, and whenever you wake, you still feel exhausted. Perhaps you can't eat. Or perhaps you keep eating. Your depression is like a weight on you, an irritant on your skin, a weight on your eyelids, a pressure on your ribs, a constant churning of the tummy.

Depression is a maladaptive behaviour utilized as a way to deal with reality. Depression is a response to trauma.

Depression is an inability to cope with the reality of the world, as our perceptions are misconceived, deeply flawed, and damaged. Thus, we can see that depression is a response to our programming and, indeed, to our drugs of approval and appreciation.

It must be said, and indeed it is often the case, that depression is the result of a singular traumatic event. If this traumatic event occurred in our adolescence or adulthood, it is natural for us to feel depressed because it is the reality of our situation. In time the depression will lift as our acceptance of the situation becomes more radical and mature, and as we learn to live life in reality, understanding and accepting what has happened.

Unfortunately, some of us are unable to do this for various different reasons, and this can lead to a lifelong depression unless we change our acceptance of our reality. We cannot change reality. We can however, change our circumstances and our perception of reality,

Most of us reading this who have experienced lifelong, deep, dark depression will know that its causes, though they may be multifarious in origin, are really of no particular concern to us. We cannot feel, we cannot motivate ourselves. We constantly blame ourselves for our lack of motivation, our failures, our inability to live life, and inability to meet the expectations of others or ourselves. We feel ashamed of how we feel, how we look, and how we act.

We feel worthless. As this feeling of worthlessness grows, we withdraw from society and those close to us, and retreat into the darkness. We exist, but we don't exist. We inhabit a twilight world, the world between despair and nothingness.

Fundamentally this is caused by our programming. Our programming from a very early age, our faulty programming. Therefore, you can see it is not your fault. Our depression is also an unanswerable craving for the drugs we need the most: approval and appreciation.

We are certain that we will never get this drug again, the approval we so badly need, and we cannot imagine life without it. We are the junkies of the sad soul.

When you are in this place, beyond meaning, beyond matters, beyond mattering then you have descended into hell.

The only way to recover and to live a life that is meaningful, rewarding, and joyful is to jettison all your programming.

You need to make a decision to understand that the drugs you crave are not real for you anymore; they never were. They are an illusion, so while you have spent your life trying to live an illusion honestly, you have obviously failed to do so.

The killer, for those of us who really know, is the complete absence of motivation, way beyond the meaning of indifference. You cannot imagine anything good ever in your life. This is fundamentally because you have been faultily programmed, and you have lived life on false assumptions.

If you want or are willing to try, even in the smallest way, to begin to live a real life, even if you fundamentally feel you are not worthy of it, then reading the 48 Acts and following the suggestions within will lead you on the only true path. It will give you information, leading to knowledge, leading to understanding, leading to awareness.

Your life, such as it is, in your own estimation is unlivable anyway. Therefore, you have nothing to lose, but you have the world to gain.

I myself was afflicted with depression for many years. Through this voyage of self-discovery, I learned how to deal with it and myself. I am not telling you to do anything; I am asking you to examine what I say and, if you wish, try to initiate it in your own life. The reward will be incredible for you.

Remember this: we who have lived in darkness for so long recognize a light, even a chink of light, when we see it, and we know it is the truth because truth is inescapable.

You will see the world in a new way, an unprogrammed way, free from your addictions and preoccupations. You will live happily.

If I have got well, then you can also.

COERCIVE CONTROL

Coercive controlling or narcissistic controlling relationships may be defined as follows:

A repeated pattern of acts of assaults, humiliation, threats, intimidation, invalidation, and any other abuse that is used to harm, punish or frighten the victim.

The overwhelming feeling of powerlessness and invalidation, and loss of confidence and self-worth, that you experience because of the actions of a narcissistic or coercive controlling personality is horrendous. It is so horrendous that you feel depersonalized. The invalidation, contempt, control, lack of freedom, and the unbelievability of your situation, all render you helpless. The person doing this to you may be your partner, child, boss, or someone else in a position of control. It could be a work colleague, fellow student, or anybody else directly connected to and associated with your life.

How does this happen to us, and why do we stay in emotionally or physically abusive relationships?

The whole immense, hidden secretive nature of coercive control and its seriously damaging effects is notoriously difficult to prove to anyone else as typically there is only one witness: you, the victim. Family members and friends may display a marked reluctance to get involved as it's 'not their business'. Alternatively, the narcissist may have weaponized those closest to you for their own ends; these people, in effect, become accomplices, or 'flying monkeys'.

These relationships destroy your social life as there is a huge amount of jealousy and control involved. The abusive partner tends to control all the financial and decision-making elements of the relationship. They do not care about the effect their savage behaviour has on their victim. Then there is the pervasive senses of foreboding and secrecy associated with these types of relationships. This is what you, as the person on the receiving end of this behaviour is constantly living with.

Intimidation, violence, isolation, and threats of law or reporting to child welfare are common, as are other threats and every kind of demeaning act imaginable.

You may or will also feel demeaned, devalued, and shamed, and eventually you will believe what the coercive controlling person tells you. That you are the lowest of the low, the scum of the earth, and utterly contemptible and worthless.

These are just some of the common effects on us when we are affected by a coercive controlling or a narcissistic person. However, what is really going on? As I have said, coercive control exists right across every social class or demographic. It is equally prevalent from the wealthiest to the poorest in society. For the purpose of explanation, I will use the example of two people in a relationship, as all other unhealthy relationships can be mirrored on this one example.

There is something else we really need to clear up here first and say it bluntly. As with everything else we have discussed, coercive controlling behaviour affects and applies equally to both men and women. The perception that this only applies to women is deeply damaging, needs to be understood clearly, and we must try and deal with it and all its permutations.

In the initial stages of the relationship, a process of 'super love' or 'love bombing' will almost always occur. The narcissistic coercive controlling person will quickly take over the relationship. They will supply superabundant love, care, attention, compliments, and everything anybody could look for.

Anyone who has been starved of love is extremely susceptible. Through their faulty programming and their addiction to the drugs of approval and appreciation, they will obviously fall for this hook, line, and sinker. They are getting approval, appreciation, acclamation, attention, adulation, affirmation, and all the things they have craved. They get an overabundant supply of their drugs.

Over a period of time the narcissistic person will gradually assume more control and will eventually direct all areas of the relationship. They will control the finances, the friends, the family, and all other affiliations.

You still don't really notice this at the beginning, as you see it as further confirmation of their love for and approval of you. The rapidity of the process and the consequences will be even worse if you have had trauma in childhood or had childhood experience of narcissistic control. You will think this is normal.

Then it gradually gets more clinging and cloying. The narcissist will monitor who you see and when you see them, and still, you will accept this as further proof of their love for you, even when they forbid you to meet with your friends or family.

They will tell you it's for your own good and that they know best. Over a period of time, things will gradually become more stultifying and controlling. It is at this point that you will start to try to assert your own individuality again. In every case this will be met by the first indications of the savage severity of what you are dealing with.

They will begin to undermine you, suggesting your friends are no good, your family is not good enough for you, and only they know the way for you to go forward. They will begin to isolate you. They will start ordering every significant event in your life, and eventually every tiny detail of your life.

You will now come to the stage where you will believe what they say. You will believe their undermining and constant devaluation. In other words, they have gaslighted you and you have started to doubt yourself. You have started to doubt reality. Having now doubted your own sanity and the reality that surrounds you, you will embark upon a series of maladaptive behaviours to counteract this or to get out of reality. However, this is merely the beginning.

You may become passive, aggressive or spiteful. You will start to have feelings of helplessness, and you will create fantasies of how life could be or will be tomorrow, when the narcissist changes. The reality is that the narcissist will never change. You may spend years trying to do everything in your power to change the narcissist. You do not realize it yet, but it is impossible to change anybody.

You may also begin to consume alcohol or drugs excessively, work excessively, or find any other form of escapism that you can. This will continue and become exponentially worse over time.

Now you have become what the narcissist has said about you all along. You have become the cause of your own ruination. This is not your fault, even though you will be continually told that it is your fault.

This is not your fault. This is caused by your faulty programming and your addiction to the drugs of approval and appreciation, and the fact that you will do anything to get them.

Now you become that which you most abhor. You are your faulty, flawed, lost outer self, craving for drugs. You become addicted to the narcissist. You become addicted to affliction.

You will begin to accept any form of bad treatment. The abnormal has become your normal. You will allow yourself to be totally invalidated. You will give up all the things you wanted to do because you will believe the narcissist when they tell you that you are not capable of doing them. You will do anything; you will abandon yourself.

Just when you imagine things could not become worse, they do, because now the narcissistic coercive controlling person will start to threaten you.

They will threaten you physically and may even use violence against you. They will threaten your life, your family's lives, and your children's lives. They will threaten you with the removal of your home and money and conduct constant character assassination. Finally, they will tell you nobody will believe you anyway.

Unfortunately, you may have already demonstrated how bad you are, in their and others' estimation, by your maladaptive behaviours. You know in your heart that what they threaten is undoubtedly true, because you know what they are capable of. They will threaten to remove you from your children, even if you have done nothing wrong, based on innuendo and sabotage.

You also know these threats are real because of another incredible tactic they have. They turn all your friends and family into 'flying monkeys'. Flying monkeys are the people who actively participate, knowingly or unknowingly, in the narcissist's smear campaign. Thus, you will be met with constant refrains such as, 'He is so good to you' and 'She is so good and nice to you, and you give her an awful time, I do not know how she puts up with you'. The narcissist will tell you, 'If you go to court, nobody will believe you'. You know that this is the truth because you cannot prove what is being done to you.

This is where you could be lucky if they physically assault you, because then you have evidence that people can see, but this evidence may still not be believed anyway. Your life will be in grave danger. You will be utterly confused. You will not be able to think straight, and you will begin to experience a feeling of hopelessness.

Know this truism: even if you give up everything in your life, every ambition, every hope, every joy, and every love, you will never appease the narcissist. Though you totally disengage from your life they will further punish you and they will never stop. The reason they cannot stop is that it is not in their nature to do so.

You will now have arrived in hell and the options are few. Suicide is the easiest way, and indeed may be your constant companion for a while. You will not be able to imagine ever having a life of joy, peace, or happiness again because of what has happened to you.

Therefore, you will not be able to imagine the scenario of leaving this person, as your self-confidence will have evaporated, and your self-worth and value will be nonexistent. This again is hopelessness, and you will begin to feel an utter lack of motivation. You will feel and know complete loneliness and that there is nobody on your side. You will be totally isolated.

This will continue until you die or leave. You may not be able to leave due to children, shared finances, a roof over your head, or other complicated entwinements.

The above scenario is one example of the many different situations in which narcissistic coercive control exists. It is to be taken as such and no more. The relationship in which you suffer this form of mental, psychological, emotional, or physical abuse may also be with a parent or grandparent, son or daughter, brother or sister, close friend, work or study colleague, employer, or indeed anybody in a position to exert a coercive controlling influence over you, or who chooses to use their authority in a coercively controlling or malevolent way. As with the other maladaptive behaviours, practices, and addictions, the 48 Acts will help you.

I know that you know what I am talking about. I know that you can identify with what I have said. This identification is all you need, because you may be completely unable to do anything else now. Your incapability may be no fault of your own; it may have been caused by what happened and is still happening to you.

You will find that initiating any process to help yourself is extremely difficult; this is also caused by trauma suffered or still ongoing. The awfulness of your situation is the cause of your lack of motivation, lack of self-confidence, and lack of self. Procrastination and utter lack of self-motivation are, believe it or not, the final remaining self-preservation attributes, or one of the last remaining forms of survival.

I implore you to follow the precepts set down in the 48 Acts not because I have said them, but because you will intuitively know and recognize their validity for you. They will change your life, from an awful existence to radically accepted reality. They will outline for you a path which you may follow. This path will give you information, knowledge, and understanding, leading to awareness.

Your constant rumination will eventually stop as will the self-recrimination. I will write a book specifically on this topic, later, for additional help, but everything you need is contained in the 48 Acts. When you follow the Acts and their way of life, your life will change beyond recognition. You will know a new life and be set free.

If I have got well, then you can too.

CHAPTER 4

WHY UNDERSTANDING IS
THE KEY TO FREEDOM

I spent most of my life running away from my history, my childhood traumas, my childhood rejection, and pain. I could not look back as it was too painful to relive the experiences.

If you wish to be well, you must first learn to see again. You must begin to see with a 'Big Seeing'. What stops you from seeing, feeling, and understanding is your addiction, your drug. I really believe it when I suggested earlier that everybody is addicted at one level or another. Some know, some don't know, some deny, and some can see no way of living without it. But make no mistake, everybody is addicted, everybody has a drug, it just depends on what you call that drug. Is it chemical dependency? Or is it an attachment? Is it a desire? The need for fame, power, glory, money, to be wanted, to be ruthless. Whatever you call it, these are drugs.

What causes you to become addicted in the first place? When you were born you were free, but very quickly you were programmed by society to behave in a certain way. Whatever society you live in, it does not matter, you will become addicted to the drugs of approval, appreciation, and belonging.

You have misunderstood all your life what love really is, what you are, and what life is. To get well you must become acquainted with what is going on and then change it. If you do not know what is going on, well, then how can you change it?

You must learn to live in the world but not be affected by it. When you become affected by what is going on all around you in the world, that leads to depression, anxiety, addiction, coercive controlling relationships, unhappiness, insecurity, and a host of other maladaptive behaviours and madness that we endure. Understand that 'being affected' is directly caused by your drugs of approval and appreciation and your programming.

We become extremely unhappy. How can this be? It is because we are addicted and programmed from birth. If we do the right thing as a child, we are a good child. If we do the wrong thing, we are a bad child, shunned, rejected. Our programming should not be about right or wrong; it should be about learning the consequences of the decisions that we make and being able to think things through for ourselves.

The good child will seek attention by being good all the time, the bad child gets attention by being bad all the time. So very quickly we learn to connect to the drugs of approval, appreciation, and attention every day for the rest of our life. There is no such thing as a bad child.

This binary, good and bad way of thinking is reinforced in your school, in your church, and in your society. Now it is exponentially reinforced through mass media and social media. The messaging is always clear and constant: conform, adhere to the messaging, accept received truths unexamined, and let somebody else think for you. We have become products of a consumerist society. We have not evolved to live this way.

You do not realize it, but every day your programming is reinforced to seek these drugs of approval and appreciation. These are your drugs; if they are withdrawn, you will crave them. This is what leads to children from a very young age becoming maladaptive in their behaviours. People in their teens seek social media and virtual friends but become ostracized and are unable to socialize and to be involved in the world.

If the drug is withdrawn by somebody that is close to you, you will do anything to get your hit of approval and appreciation. Equally and increasingly, large corporate structures hold the power to manipulate and control the drugs you most crave.

We are in a most invidious position. We need, as individuals and as a society, to unite behind a common ideal. Through our many millions of years of evolution, we cannot willfully wish away our nature, or hope that we are a highly emotionally advanced society living in a peaceful utopia. However, we are very clever and have survived when all other hominids have been wiped out by us or the evolutionary process. Our greatest hope of survival, initially, is to change who the enemy is.

To do this we must get information which leads to knowledge, which will lead to understanding, which will lead to awareness.

It is with the hope and earnest wish to improve your life and the life of others that I present the 48 Acts. I know that they will help you become free from your drugs of approval and appreciation and your programming, so that you can instead participate in life in all its wonder and glory, unafraid and free.

PART II
THE 48 ACTS

THE SIXTEEN AXIOMS

1. Life Is Full of Suffering.
2. Your Life Is Not About You.
3. There Is a Power Greater than You.
4. You Have Everything You Need at your Disposal to be Happy; You Just Don't Know it.
5. Your Suffering is Caused by Your Programming. The Key to Unlocking Your Programming is Knowledge, Understanding, and Awareness.
6. Trauma is Caused by your Perception of Circumstances.
7. Bad Thinking, Bad Feelings, and Trauma and Pain Cause Damaging Responses in You, Leading You to Ever Greater Life-Changing Reaction Events, Pain, and Suffering.
8. Addiction and Maladaptive Behaviours are a Response to Trauma and Pain.
9. After Becoming Sufficiently Unwell, You Will Feel Compelled to Do Something About it, Because You Have Begun to Realize That the Problem is in You.
10. You Decide to Act and Take Responsibility for Your Own Life. This Will Empower You as You Paradoxically Realize That Powerless-

ness, be it Over People, Events, or Situations, Leads You to an Acceptance Which Leads You to Self-Empowerment and Peace of Mind.

11. You Come to the Realization That You Cannot Change Anybody
Else. You Will Stop Ruminating and Living in Your Head, and Start
Living in Reality, No Longer Thinking About How Things Should be,
But Accepting How Things are in Reality.

12. You Come to the Realization That it is You Who Must Change.

13. Working on a Programme of Self-Knowledge and Self-Examination, You Accept Who You Are, Good and Bad.

14. You Will Wake up and Become Aware. By Becoming Aware, You
Can See All Things as They Really Are, and See Yourself and Your
Right to Exist. You Will See the Nature of All Things.

15. Through Knowledge and Awareness You Will Discern That There
is a Power Greater Than You. That You can Know This Power In Your
Reality and not as a Mental Concept

16. You Will Have a God, Not of Your Own Imagining, But of Reality.

THE SIXTEEN FALSE BELIEFS

1. You Cannot Be Happy Without the Things That You Are Attached to and That You Believe to be all-Important.
2. You Believe Happiness is in the Future: When You Get a New House, Career, or Relationship, or when you achieve Fame or Wealth.
3. You Are Your Feelings. If You feel Anger, Resentment, Fear, Disappointment, and Shame, These Feelings Justify Your Behaviours.
4. If You Feel Anger, Disappointment, Resentment, Fear, Shame, etc., Because of What Somebody Else Said or Did to you, these feelings Justify Your Behaviour.
5. In Order to Cease Your Maladaptive Behaviours and Addictions, You Must Constantly Identify with Others Who Have Done So, Instead of Emulating What They Have Accomplished on Their Journey to Date.
6. You Must Cease Your Maladaptive Behaviours and Addictions on the Instigation of Others.
7. You Will be Happy if You Can Change Others, Or If The People Closest to You Change.
8. Happiness is in Things, People, Possessions, and The World Outside.

9. If You Change Everything You Have, and Achieve Everything You Wish to Do, You Will be Happy.

10. If All Your Desires are Fulfilled and All Your Dreams Come True, Then You Will be Happy.

11. If Your Love Depends on Others, and You Cling to Them and Control Them in a Cage of Love, You Will be Happy.

12. If You Follow Your Religion, Beliefs, or Ideology with Great Zeal, Then You Will be Happy.

13. If you Sacrifice Everything for Others, Including Your Career, All Your Possessions, and Aspirations, You Will be Happy.

14. The Three Core Beliefs:

What Does Not Kill You Makes You Weaker.

You Are Your Feelings.

The World is Made up of Either Good or Bad People.

15. Fear, Worry, Anxiety, Loneliness, Sorrow, Vulnerability, Pain, and Many More Afflictions are Not a Part of Successful Living and Should be Hidden and Suppressed.

16. Your Life is a Shambles and You Are Blindly and Robotically Participating in Life, Without Ever Thinking of Why You Do What You Do.

THE SIXTEEN KEY ACTIONS

1. You Have Come to the Realization That All is Not Well in Your Life. Whether This May be due to Addiction, Depression, Anxiety, Controlling or Toxic Relationships, Named or Unnamed fears, or Trauma or Resentful Dissatisfaction, You are Unhappy and Your Life is Spiraling out of Control.
2. You Admit That You do not Understand The Reason Why Your Life is Like This; Or, if You do think you understand, You are probably wrong.
3. You Realize That You Are Living an Inauthentic Life, and That You are Unaware and Lack the Ability to Live in the World.
4. You Resolve to Empower Yourself Through Self-Knowledge.
5. You Resolve to Seek This Knowledge No Matter What the Cost.
6. You Have Come To The Realization That:

> Life is Full of Suffering.
> Your Life is Not About You.
> There is a Power Greater Than You.

7. You Come to See That Knowledge, Leading to Understanding, Will Lead You to Awareness.

8. With Complete Honesty You Examine All Your Behaviours and Maladaptive Practices, Identifying All those That are Leading to Self-harm, Destruction, and Unhappiness.

9. You Decide to Change All Harmful Behaviours.

10. You Resolve to Leave The Past Behind, as it Now Has No Power Over You. You Cease to Identify With It, And Instead Live in the Present, Looking Forward to a Happy Future.

11. You Take Responsibility for all of Your Actions Past and Present, Irrespective of What They are, and Cease to Blame Others. You Decide to get Rid of all Resentments, Justified or Unjustified, Seeing Them for the Poison of the Soul That They Really Are.

12. You Resolve to Become Your True, Integrated, Authentic Self. Endeavoring as Much as Possible, in a Thoughtful way, to Make Good the Harm You Have Caused to Others.

13. You Learn Unconditional Acceptance of How You Were, what Happened to You, How you Hurt Others, and How You Were Hurt by Others; You Forgive both Yourself and Them.

14. You Continue to Work Every Day on Yourself and Practice Self-reflection. You Realize the Divine Spark of Greatness Within You. You Learn to Love Yourself as You Truly Are, Accepting That Inalienable Love and Truth are in the World.

15. Having Gained Much Greater Understanding and Realizing That There is a Force Much Greater Than Ourselves, Perceive That This Power Will Help Us When all Else Fails, If We Just Ask. Having Known so Much Pain and Trauma, We Know That Humility in Itself is Not Humiliation. Thus, We Will Loose the Chains That Bind Us, and We Will be Set Free.

16. Get Into Reality, Become Aware.

THE 48 ACTS
THE SIXTEEN AXIOMS

LIFE IS FULL OF SUFFERING

You will begin at the beginning. On your journey through these 48 Acts you will discover and understand yourself and your place in the world. You will understand your society and the world you live in. You will see through the many mistaken assumptions and false beliefs that you have and hold, and, crucially, understand why you have them.

Thus, over a period of time you will learn how to lose unhappiness, addictions, and depressions, and all the unsatisfactory ways of living that you feel you must do. You will learn to live and grow, enjoying life to the full no matter the circumstances. You will be able to be self-accountable. You will take responsibility for your own life and see a new way to live, free and unfettered.

These 48 Acts are laid out sequentially, so it is best to begin at the beginning. Sometimes the same idea may be repeated across different acts. There is a reason for this. I have found from personal experience that though I may hear a thing a thousand times, I may only understand it on the thousand and first time. Seek only clarity of understanding, not confrontation and division, which are frankly a waste of time.

Examine everything I say in your heart, taking nothing for granted, finding your own way to understand it in yourself. Together we can make this journey. Together we can live our allotted time in existence emancipated and free. We will count no price too high to free ourselves from our afflictions once and for all, and thus we will know the value of that which we gain in freedom.

Thus, we begin.

We need to understand that the short sentence defining Act One, 'Life is Full of Suffering', is interwoven throughout the human experience. It is true. It is reality. Our greatest tragedy is that we are unable to accept this self-evident truth. In other words, we refuse to accept reality. Let us therefore dive in and examine and dissect this truth so that we may gain a greater understanding.

What do we mean by suffering, or how can we define suffering?

On the one hand we have natural events that cause suffering: earthquakes, natural disasters, diseases, and all the things that are a part of the world. Death is a part of this process, although we try to gloss over it and call it something else like 'passing over' or 'passing on', because in our delusion we refuse to accept it.

On the other hand, we have 'caused suffering'. This is suffering caused by us humans. It is caused by, but not exclusive to war, famine, corruption, violence, rape, and all of the personal hurts we inflict on other people. All of these and more, too numerous to mention, cause suffering. Sometimes these can overlap; for example, a famine can be caused by a natural event, but be subsequently manipulated by us to ethnically cleanse an already devastated area. All these actions are caused by humans.

A third suffering we are subjected to is internal suffering. Mental pain can be the worst of all. We can also say that this suffering is caused by our perception of things. Thus, we say the familiar refrains, 'Life is so unfair', 'The world owes me something', 'Why am I poor or sick and have nothing while some are very rich?', and countless others.

Everywhere we look we can see unfairness which causes suffering. Many people could say, 'I am sick and in very poor circumstances. Yet other people who have lived debauched and hedonistic lives, they did not get sick nor are they poor. It is so very unfair, and this causes me suffering.'

We need to distinguish what suffering really means.

Suffering is endemic to the human condition. We cannot deny it and although we may not like it, suffering is often our greatest teacher.

We can see that many causes of suffering are natural occurrences. We also need to understand that a lot of our suffering is caused by our own actions and by the actions of others.

Therefore, it is reasonable to conclude that our refusal to accept suffering as a part of our human existence is the greatest cause of fear in us. We have moved into unreality.

We are born happy.

We are born happy, uncluttered, and unprogrammed. It is all the things that we have subsequently done in our lives that have made us unhappy. We have happiness within us, uncaused and free, but we refuse to see this; we are unable to see this because of our childhood development and the programming inherent in the process of becoming unhappy.

If we examine the last number of years, we can see that we have been dealing with pandemics, wars, and the ever-increasing potential to destroy our planet in a number of ways either through a nuclear holocaust, through the stupidity of humans who create a virus that can't be cured, or through climate change.

Unfortunately, there are many other existential problems coming down the track for us. These problems are the sickness and sadness of individual humans, the proliferation of addictions, depression, fear, and anxieties that grip the hearts of most individuals in our current age.

Our greatest problem is that we refuse to accept where we are Compounding the issue, we are under the impression that we can ameliorate or trade the consequences of these events in different ways. We can bargain, we can manipulate, we can have short-term thinking, and we can obfuscate. All of this is at best useless, or at worst dangerous and potentially fatal for everyone on this planet, including you.

Programming

In our programming, from a very early age, we are told that we will be happier if we have more things. Thus, we have consumerism, materialism, capitalism, and commercialism in which we buy things to try to make us happier. This is the macrocosm. This pervades every facet of modern existence, practically everywhere on the planet.

The microcosm is a reduction of this way of life and being to just you. If you give yourself more things, and indulge in a life of pleasure, excess, and openness to external things, you will be happy and you will not need to suffer. You will assuage your suffering. Suffering will not be real for you. It is veritably the age of the 'ode to the selfish self'.

Unfortunately, the capitalist, consumer, multinational organizations and their media reinforce this message every day. They use our fear of suffering (which is really a deep-rooted malaise, and a complete lack of understanding) to manipulate and to fool us. Most of the things that we buy are not necessities but are things that we feel we must buy in order to be happy.

This leads us to the conclusion that you can assuage your unhappiness by buying and having external things. We have fallen into this trap; we misunderstand. It is not our fault, because we have been given the wrong information.

The world is full of suffering, but we have been programmed to think it is not, or that we can ameliorate it in foolish ways. The logical consequence of this way of thinking is that we become ingrained with the false belief that we are meaningless anyway, that we are just a byproduct of chance, of accident. We are the result of a quantum fluctuation. This is the great lie you will hear, the most insidious falsehood promulgated in and perpetrated on our age that life and existence are meaningless, that we are accidents of fate, and that everything is pointless.

We have this false ideology of meaningless blasted right across our world. Everywhere we work, rest, or play, we are bombarded by those in control of commerce, media, and social media that the only way to relieve our meaningless suffering is to buy more of their product. Even our art, music, and culture reflect this new age of meaninglessness, this age of unreality. Our scientists have become the new acolytes and high priests of the modern age, the age of disbelief.

We must learn to distinguish between individual suffering and societal suffering. If we lack the capacity to distinguish between the two, we will inexorably continue to experience a rapid decline of the self, the planet, and all who are on it. We will have the entropic and exponential destruction of civilization. We also need to see that individual and societal suffering are completely intertwined. Though we are products of society and the programming inherent in it, unless we evolve and grow as individuals we will continue our errant path, whistling unknowingly toward our own oblivion.

Think about the following statement:

If there were no humans in the world, would there be good or evil?

Just think about it.

We are a society on a large dose of a sedative or some other form of drug. We are sleepwalking.

We take more tablets, we buy and consume more products, we watch more TV and cable news. We live on and by social media to distract ourselves from reality and to assuage a hunger that we cannot satisfy, partly because we don't know the cause of the hunger. Often, we do not realize that it is there in the first place.

It is inescapably true that over the course of the centuries, as a society we have become more addicted. We are an addictive race.

You and I have been trained to be addicted to the most powerful drug there is. The most powerful drug that has ever existed, much more powerful than alcohol, chemical drugs, or any behavioral drug. You have been trained to become addicted to the drug of approval and appreciation.

You could also call this drug by its other brand names: praise, acceptance, prosperity, validation, and vindication — and just like any other alcoholic or drug addict, you can now be controlled by your supplier.

How did this happen?

As civilization developed and grew from our nomadic heritage and set down ever-stronger roots, our way of life changed radically. We spent millions of years living in a holistic, natural way, at one with the environment, but that is unsuitable for our new way of living.

We now live in close proximity with many thousands of others in a hierarchical structure with much more clearly defined, specialized roles within the new society. Therefore, we can see that the hierarchy's rules, regulations, and control are a part of our evolutionary process. We can also see that these imposed, rigorous, demarcated rules and structures arrived very late in terms of our evolution and natural selection. It was, perforce, the only way to control our strong territorial and killer instincts. It was the only game in town that would work. It was the only way we as *homo sapiens* could manage to coexist relatively peacefully. Natural selection and circumstances forced us to create 'super tribalism' to survive.

We took what was good about our clan and tribal structure, finessed over millions of years, and in making the new super tribalism we gained a lot. We also lost a lot.

This process began approximately twelve thousand years ago. Our natural habitat and way of living for millions of years was, as we have seen, based on clans or extended family groups. Each tribe or clan had a maximum of a hundred and fifty individuals. This was the most that the clan or tribe could handle. When a significant surplus beyond this critical limit occurred, it caused an immediate splinter effect, with effectively the creation of a separate tribe in a new territory.

It is a remarkable macrocosmic version of cell division. The new cell colonizes new territory. Thus, similarly, we spread and spread and spread. We are tribal by survival evolution. It was an essential component of our evolution. It is in our genes. It was there for millions of years. This is really important to remember.

Our first settlements and subsequent development of cities quickly became far more populous than our small tribe or clan settlements. Thus control over individuals and society became necessary, so that we would not kill each other, but instead work cohesively in a larger unit.

We constructed and concocted new methods of control that had not existed previously. One of the consequences of this was that instead of knowing the god or gods of our experience, we started to believe in a god of our own creation, the god of our own manipulation.

Thus, by an evolutionary sleight of hand, we created our own ultimate arbiter. The ability to appeal to a higher authority or in this case the ultimate authority, God himself, is the ideal solution. Power then divests automatically from on high to his earthly representative or representative class. This also obviates any dissent and imbues the possessors of this authority with an unimpeachable and indeed unapproachable mystique.

Thus, the hierarchical, authoritarian, and all-powerful elite class was born organically. There really is no mystery about it, and it is important for us to understand this so that we may see how we as individuals and as a society have arrived where we are today.

The next thing that is very important for us to understand is something very noteworthy and special about us as humans. Though I discuss this in much greater detail in the book *The Wheel of Life*, it is essential I summarize this one incredibly important feature of our species.

From the beginning of the science of modern paleoanthropology to the recent genomic sequencing discoveries, we can conclusively state one hugely significant fact about us: we are the only species of hominid left on the planet. We descended from the first real identifiable hominid (Australopithecus) approximately five million years ago, and we have subsequently made all other rivals extinct. We achieved this through our composite opposing attributes, namely violence and intelligence. Fundamentally, however, we achieved our survival, domination, ascendency, and technological advances through our ability to cooperate very effectively with each other and as a group.

Full square beside group cooperation is group need for control of territory. This surpasses every other drive in humans, be it sex, belonging, attraction, or any other cohesive element of our tribe or our clan. Territory is everything.

This key understanding explains so much about us as individuals and as a society, and it seems inescapably true that the need for territory is as strong among us today as it ever was.

War is everywhere, again.

Territory is an ever-scarcer commodity. This situation plus the vast population growth has led to ever more dangerous conflicts and wars. If we are not careful, the lust for land will wipe us out.

The problem for us is that we as individuals are subconsciously aware of this disquiet, whether we know it or not. The constant unease and anxiety created by these escalating wars and strife are causing in us, individually and collectively, a great unnamed fear.

A mere twelve thousand years of 'civilisation' has had very little effect on this savage, primitive need and instinct. When you see and understand this, then all of the conflict in the modern world is very easily intelligible. We are, in all our glory, despite all our artistic, musical, and scientific accomplishments and our medical and societal advances, just at best advanced stone age people. In reality we are *homo sapiens* with the primitive instincts of our ancestors. These ancestors had great awareness of their place in the world and life. We seem to have gradually lost all this awareness.

We have to accept this fact even though it is abhorrent to our modern ears. We succeeded because we are merciless. We brook no opposition; we wipe them out. We defend our territory as our primary motivation, and we kill all intruders.

On this I assure you there can be no ambivalence: territory is the primary driver of our species. If we couple this primary need for territory with our created organic god, then we can see this is not a god or reality at all. It is a construct. Through the divestment of power from this false god to his priests, kings, acolytes, and so forth, the inescapable conclusion is obvious as follows.

We have been controlled by ruling classes since we first became domesticated. Kings and God Kings. Their hierarchy, their functionaries, their minions, their bureaucracy and their civil and religious control. In other words, their ideology. Now if you incorporate into this the programming that has been created around us as individuals from our earliest age, then you will see just how we are where we are. Why? Our programming has made us, as I have said, addicted to the most powerful drugs ever known to humans, namely, approval and appreciation. The craving for these drugs has us in the mess we are in. The biggest problem is that rulers and elites have in effect been our biggest supplier. They are our drug pushers. We are still controlled. Think it out.

The Individual

You, as an individual, have become abducted by and addicted to the drug of approval; you need to get it. Thus, if you do not get it, you feel rejected, and you feel more terrible and more consumed by cravings than any drug addict.

If you don't get the house that you want, the car you want, the job you want, or whatever else (the list is endless), you feel rejected, deeply unhappy. These are all 'caused' things.

Equally, if you don't feel excited or stimulated, you feel unhappy and you go and look for more social media, more TV. This is because you cannot bear to be with yourself or to feel the realities of life, as you do not want to be in reality. I never wanted to be in reality.

If we choose the postmodernist, consumerist, capitalist view of the world in which we all live, the inescapable conclusion is that that there is no ultimate moral imperative. Life is meaningless. We are accidents. We arrived under the veil of quantum mechanics. There is no point or purpose, there is no good and no evil. There is no right or wrong. There is no truth, or there are alternate versions of truth.

If we look at these ideas with openness, knowledge, understanding, and awareness, we might see that this is a flawed argument. We can look at the origins of Hitler's Germany and the consequences of war and the Holocaust. Mao caused the deaths of ninety million individuals in China, Stalin killed millions in the Soviet Union. America's constant wars have killed many native peoples and destroyed cultures. Examples are the war in Vietnam and the utter destruction of Cambodia, Afghanistan, Iraq, and so on. We can see England and the British Empire, and the dreadful consequences of their actions on all the colonized nations and their people, including my own country. We therefore ask, 'Who caused this?' Humans vying for power, delusional in their beliefs.

Yet it was Hitler's view that it was scientifically appropriate to exterminate the Jews because it was his own German people's right to do so, as the Germans were the superior race, the supreme race. He was underpinned in this view by almost two thousand years of Christian thinking. Christians believed in the utter moral reprehensibility of the Jews since they had 'murdered' Jesus Christ.

This extremely erroneous world view underpins the Soviet Union, Stalin and the communist ideology and its consequences. Likewise with the Americans who wiped out the native population because they viewed them as 'savages.'

We do not need a god to make us bad; we do it by ourselves. We do not need a god to make us hate; we do it by ourselves. We are the cause of our own suffering, and most of the time we do not know it.

We are completely unaware and ignorant of all but the most primitive of things.

Thus, we can extrapolate from this that you, as an individual, believe and accept what you are told by postmodern cultural consumerism. There is no external or absolute morality. Morality is only what is decided by people in power.

You can see that this way of thinking has been the case all through history. We can get any god to do what we want him to do, and we can kill very well on his behalf. He kills because we make him do so. In war, our side and the other side have diametrically opposing needs and ideologies, yet each side claims god is on their side and that their morality is better. Everybody dies.

The world is in a very sick place

You can see from all of this that the world is in a very sick place. This is the end product of twelve thousand years of manipulation, twelve thousand years of programming, and twelve thousand years of creating a sick society, and we are getting exponentially sicker.

The world is full of suffering that we can now see. The world is full of suffering that is caused both by circumstances and by us humans; fundamentally, the world is also full of suffering because of our perceptions and our addiction to the drugs of approval and appreciation. Our first Act is to see that this is so. To understand how this could be so. To see that suffering is the way of the world. To understand.

ACT TWO AXIOMS
YOUR LIFE IS NOT ABOUT YOU

Your life is not about you; it really isn't. This misconception is where I think most of our problems begin. Everywhere you look, everywhere you are, you are incessantly bombarded with the message 'It is all about you', be it on TV, books, cinema, magazines, social media, advertisements. The repetition of this message is endless. This is what we are misunderstanding.

If it is all about me, then I have a small life divorced from reality, one in which it is all about me, my preferences, my wants, my needs, my opinions, my guilt, my shame, my group, my everything. It is all about me. This is a very small life. This is a false, outer life.

I can justify anything. I can justify any of my actions, because they are just based on my needs. Therefore I can justify war, I can justify killings, I can justify bad behaviour. This is not good for me or anybody else because I cannot see that this is a false self. When this justification is taken to its extremes, you can see that you can feel good about yourself while chasing the next fix your whole life. Everything becomes about chasing the next fix in the end. If you are in a position of power, you can justify anything while claiming that 'God is on my side', and in this way you can temporarily feel good about yourself.

You can justify your actions, but you will never be happy. You will never know contentment, you will just know brief fixes, or interludes until you must go and chase the next fix. I am not saying that an outer life is bad, because it is not. It is necessary for us to interact in the world and with our fellows. It's what makes us strive and achieve. The problem is that we end up believing that this is all there is.

This is where we have all been led astray into unreality. This is not the way it is meant to be at all, and we can all see when we use a bit of honesty that we have been manipulated into this way of thinking for the last fifty to sixty years, especially now that we do not even know what the truth is any more.

Our first job is to identify that this small needy self, full of self-pity, self-justification, self righteousness, anger, guilt, shame, and rage, is a small life. We need to realize that if you live like this, you will die like this, and you will die as nothing. You will be dead; you will be gone.

Those of us who have suffered a lot, either through addiction, trials and tribulations, or maladaptive behaviours, know the extremities of pain and suffering more than most other people as we have sunk to a very low place. In a strange sense, we have an advantage over others in that we have begun to see the end of the road. The problem is that we cannot see the light; we see no hope. We see no hope because we have lived a life of falseness, of unreality, where we have fully believed the message 'It is all about you'. We have seen it through to the very end and to the obvious ultimate conclusion that this message is illusory, that it cannot possibly bring you happiness. It only brings you misery, unimaginable suffering, and pain.

It also makes you think, in a fatalistic way, 'What is the point of it all?' We are just chaff on the breeze, and the propaganda emanating now from certain sectors of science and the media is 'well, we are all here just by chance anyway', therefore 'everything is pointless, so you should buy my product, it will make you feel better about yourself for a little while'.

Wake up, this is a lie.

When you look at all the major religions, philosophies from our

earliest written history, and oral tradition, certain things emerge.
Listen to or read about what the mystics have said. They all agree on
certain points irrespective of religion, ideology, or civilisation. The
similarities between them is amazing.

Our recorded history is only about seven thousand years old. Our
oral traditions date much further back into the mists of time. The
dawn of civilization began, and with the establishment of the first
city-states we began to live in close proximity with one another in
high population densities for the very first time. Uruk, considered the
earliest city-state, was first settled in approximately 5000 BCE. This is
when all the rules changed.

Because all the rules changed, we learned to programme and be
programmed in a new way. If we are to become happy, to get well, we
must learn that life is not about us, the little self. It is about us, the
true self, the real self, so we need to define what the real self is. We
need to define who we truly are. Most of us do not have any idea who
we truly were before we were programmed and before we became
identified by labels like doctor, nurse, solicitor, laborer, criminal,
addict, TV presenter, or whatever other appendage you care to use to
describe yourself. These occupations are not who you are; these are
just attachments of what you have done or what you are doing. We
make the mistake of thinking that they are us, but they are not.

While not looking back to a bucolic, primaeval past in a foolishly
mythic or idealized way, it is true that we as humans were more aware
of and participatory in our true nature before we became 'civilised' or
sedentary. This is how we successfully evolved over the eons. Therefore, this is who we were before we began to live in towns and cities;
that is the way we were born in reality.

Similarly, the true self is who we are on the inside, devoid of attachments and appellations. The core of our reality. The real you. This is
uncaused. There is nothing you can do to alter it. This is who you really
are. What you can do is feed it, let it grow. First you need to become aware
that your central reality exists. The quest of our lives is to find out who we
are in reality, to see who we really are as people and as individuals in soci-

ety, and to accept our true selves. There is a price you have to pay for this. There is a price for enlightenment, for knowing, for unity with the essence, for understanding, and that is: 'You must die to yourself'.

But what does this mean? Firstly, it must be said that there is a great deal of pseudoscience, psycho babble, pseudotherapy, and new age nonsense surrounding anything that is not corporeal or empirically verifiable. We have lost all rational options of dealing with our inner selves in a meaningful way. We have lost the connection, the ability, and the language. We have lost our awareness. Instead, we have built a huge industry of 'wellness' in which we try to deal with ourselves and our reality by resorting to crystals, angels, and a whole host of well-meaning but uninformed people who are promoting a panacea that can never work.

What does it really mean to die to yourself? What does it really mean to feed the inner you and die to the outer you? Fundamentally, it means that you must die to the little self, so that you can become alive to the big, real self.

There are many many stories throughout our history, going back to our oldest myths and traditions, that convey essentially this same message. One example that immediately comes to mind was given by Jesus in the Christian Bible. Whether you take this as ancient literature or actual dogma, the essence and pertinence of the message remain the same.

'Very truly, I tell you, unless a grain of wheat falls into the earth and dies, it remains just a single grain; but if it dies, it bears much fruit.' (John 12:24 NRSV)

The first way we can liberate the inner self is through some mystical event or experience. Through the word, through art , music or an encounter with beauty. The outer self realizes its own limitation, in time and place. We have an encounter with the Truth.

This shows us that the small self must die to allow the big self to grow. The false self cannot die or lose its hold over us and cannot give up its attachment to unreal, temporal things until an essential change takes place, in us. Understand that once having become enmeshed, mired, buried in misery and suffering, we will feel we have to do something or die. We will feel compelled to act.

The second way is that we will have some sort of experience that lifts us out of unreality, but unfortunately this life-changing event occurs very rarely indeed. The third way is to understand with knowledge and awareness. The truth and reality will reveal itself to you. Therefore, you have to die to yourself, to let go of the ego and false self so that you can live life anew. Live life with a bigger understanding, a proper understanding in reality, a big feeling, where you can be compassionate, forgiving, and always looking to who you can help, not who can help you.

The little self will always find those who are just like you, with the same ethnicity, color, beliefs, social status, group identity, etc. The big self will always see in a new way that is devoid of rancor, anger and hate, giving the feeling and the understanding that all are one. The new understanding will show us that all our feelings have the energy, the spark, of essence.

Increasingly, as we become a sicker society, we can observe tribalism saturating the media, both mass media and social media. 'They are doing something to us'. 'We need to take our power, control, and country back'.

We are now so sick that if we do not stop we will all become like every addict, terminal in our decline. We will be forgotten, and we will as individuals and as a society blow away on the breeze of nothingness.

The false self is not real; it is an illusion, it is a construct. If this is all you have, then you have nothing. If this is a summary of you and your life, then you have nothing.

Make no mistake in understanding this. I am not saying the false, outer self is bad, for it is certainly not. It is the self that drives you to study, work, compete, have relationships, and interact with the world in a general way. It's just very limited. That is as far as it takes you. The outer self is very binary in nature. Things are black or white in this dualistic way of thinking. There are no gray areas. There are no nuances. I am right, you are wrong. If my ideology is right then obviously yours is wrong. You can see where that gets us. It is a very binary, dualistic system developed especially strongly since we formed the first city-states and developed a structured proximal society. The outer self is what dies when you die. It is the self that also causes us so much pain and destruction.

All material things are temporal. If you do not develop the inner self, then you are destined to live a very limited, small, and controlled life. It becomes a life of nonparticipation in the wonder of life, but concerned with all the problems of life because these are all that can be seen. As the old adage says: 'You cannot see the wood for the trees'.

Unfortunately, this is where the misery comes from: the helplessness, the hopelessness of life. People will honestly believe that it is all pointless, all meaningless, all nothing; life is transient. People don't matter, nothing matters. It is only you the little you that matters. The little false self. This is people's truth. This 'truth' makes us sick. We can believe any 'reality we like'. Sadly, those of us who have experienced the full rigors of addiction can see the consequences of believing a false truth or narrative for years more than most. We are experts on it. Most 'ordinary people' are equally addicted, they are equally delusional in their false belief. They are completely unaware of this.

This situation is not our fault, it is not your fault and in a way it is not anybody's fault. It is the way we have evolved as a society, and as a society we must change, or we will cease to exist.

The real self (when we begin to see and to know it, either through pain and suffering or through some sort of enlightening or mystical experience) is the only self that really matters. We can then see that a life constructed around and by the false self, where everything is all about us, is pure illusion. You have a choice either to continue to live in unreality or to learn to live in the reality of the world.

The world of reality is bathed with the power of love, the power of the universe, the power of the essence. This is you as you are, becoming aware of who you really are. As I said, those of us who have come through great suffering have an advantage. If your life is miserable, or if you have no peace of mind, you are addicted. If you are feeling hopeless, depressed, not in control in relationships, or just a general malaise, then you will see the beginning of truth in this.

You must divest yourself of the false self and get into the true self, the real self. When you get into reality, into your true self, you won't have the ups and downs, the rollercoaster of emotions. You won't have the need to blot out feelings that you think you cannot cope with, because you will learn how to handle all feelings. You will handle any situation that presents itself when you learn that your life is not about the little you, but the bigger you.

You will not feel or adhere to tribal ideologies. You will see ideologies and identify them for what they really are; you will see the real. You will see that all are one, all the rest are illusionary, let go of it all.

We must die to ourselves before we die, so that we are not afraid to die, and when we die our first death we die to ourselves as the little I, but we become alive to ourselves the big I, the true I, the real I. Therefore have courage. Change. Plant the seed. Let the seed die so you can eat of the fruit of the plant that grows from your seed.

ACT THREE AXIOMS
THERE IS A POWER GREATER
THAN YOU

'There is a power greater than you'. What does that mean, and how does it help me in my life?

It is self-evident that there is a power greater than us in a physical sense. If we look at the universe, stars, and galaxies we can see that there is a vast physical power and presence much greater than ourselves. Is that what we mean? Yes and No.

First of all, let me start off by saying that whenever most people today see the words 'power greater than myself', 'God', or any other such appellations, they become either indifferent, annoyed, or very angry. They do not take what is said seriously if it is in any way connected with a higher power or 'god stuff'. You cannot blame people for this reaction. So let us look at the religious aspect of the wording 'a power greater than ourselves' and its negative connotations.

We can see straight away if we begin by looking at the Judeo-Christian value system. The Christian church was seen as the apotheosis or climax of all human life on earth, past, present, and future. God comes on earth to free all from sin and all human frailties. It was the ultimate message of love and self-sacrifice. The good news really embodied Act 2. This promise of hope began on the premise of a

nonjudgemental message: do no harm to anybody, love your neighbor, do no violence, give all you have away. It really is the ultimate
message of inclusivity and community. All were welcome and all
were equal. Judge nobody, but love all. Love yourself. How rapidly it
diverged from this original message.

Yes indeed, this is how it started off, full of hope and joy. There
would be no more tribalism or war, but all would be united as one in
the message of love, one great world tribe group. Well.....if this
powerful idea was proclaimed in our present world by some brave
individual, then , most assuredly this individual would be branded a
communist and a new world order conspiracist terrorist and
locked up.

What went wrong?

In essence we mistook the messengers for the message.

We believed in hierarchy and those 'chosen' to lead us. We did
this because it is all we have ever known since we became 'civilized'.
Fundamentally we must understand that our blind belief in hierarchies, systems, governments, kings and all other systems and institutions run by men has led us to our present crisis, our crisis of
unbelief. With the advent of modern technology, we have finally seen
that all these systems are flawed. They all lie, cheat, murder, control
and destroy. Now we as a society are moving to what we perceive as
the only logical conclusion...we believe nobody, nothing. Everything
is a lie. Even the world itself is probably a hologram and most of the
leaders or governments may not even be human or if they are, well
they are not there for our benefit. When we understand this outcome
and why, then a lot of the modern world begins to make more sense.

What subsequently happened is radically important for us to
understand. Therefore, we need to dive straight in. All ideas, however
powerful, are filtered through the ideologies and perceptions of those
who receive them, the converted. Thus the essence of the idea, over
time becomes watered down and changed to fit the culture of whatever community receives it. The Christian church changed from its
humble and pure beginnings to being the church of empire. The
Roman emperor Constantine, in 313 BCE made Christianity the offi-

cial religion of the Roman empire, and all that that entails. Everything now changes. Subsequent to this event, the Christian church, and the Catholic church, have been responsible for the deaths of millions of people in the name of religion. Since followers can claim to have God on their side, they can feel good about it, feel justified in murdering other people who do not conform or belong to their ideology or religion. How did this happen so quickly? How could we kill so well in the name of love?

Christian ideology treated women appallingly reverting to an Old Testament and pagan dogma. This was despite the significantly advanced position of women in early Christianity (for its time). The pervasive misogynistic underpinnings of our culture stem from, and in many ways are underpinned by, the edicts and dogma disseminated by the Christian church. Any close examination of the origin story of Christianity will thus show this misogyny is completely unjustified and was added in later. The same Christian value system with its binary world view of them and us, we are right so therefore everybody else is wrong led us to perpetrate the horror of the Holocaust. We are right and superior; the rest are wrong and inferior. It's very easy. Think. Have we really changed?

In the recent past, though not for the first time, the Roman Catholic church has been involved in sex scandals, particularly child abuse, on a worldwide scale. To compound this, it has engaged in unrelenting cover-ups. At the same time, it has presented a very hypocritical line on children's rights, women's rights, gender rights, and the rights of ordinary believers. It has become an exclusionary, judgmental institution. This 'correct' view is so endemic in the general population that the very name 'God' or 'Jesus Christ' is enough to incense people, to drive them into angry outbursts and rage. Based on the evidence, this reaction is fully justified.

If we look at Evangelical Christians, we can see the emotional manipulation of people, primarily for the maximum extraction of money from the most vulnerable, promising them a 'gateway into heaven'. But only if enough money is paid to the earthly gate keepers. The weak and susceptible, genuinely looking for a way to cope in this world, to survive, to win the heavenly lottery and the cynical exploiters.

If we look at radical Islam, we can see its total intolerance of other religions, its war foundation, and its control of its followers. Once again this is very illustrative to us so that we may understand. Islam contains such beautiful and noble ideals. In the early Middle Ages, it was an extraordinary society. Islamic communities and societies were foremost in the world in a wide array of human innovations and developments. Islam developed the most advanced medicine, the most advanced mathematics and physics. It developed the wonderful poetry of so many great poets including Rumi and extraordinarily beautiful music. The greatest mystics were Islamic such as Ibn Arabi. It was a golden age of progress.

What went wrong? Simply put, the secular and religious leaders issued edicts forbidding all exploration of these areas of human interest and advancement. Why? It was against the religion. The real reason was their own insecurities and their need for control. Thus, we can see that when something is stunted, be it a whole world view or an individual, it remains in the trauma and the timeframe of when the hurt occurred. Nothing grows.

Hinduism is an ancient religion. The word itself is a general term for a diverse and multifaceted series of different belief systems based on the same basic ideals. These ideals and beliefs are truly beautiful. Everything in the universe is God's. Each person is intrinsically divine, and life's purpose is to find this divinity within and to realise this divinity in all others. The Hindu faith is totally non exclusionary, and all are welcome. The reality, unfortunately, is very different. The caste system. The same wars and injustices as all other belief systems.

Buddhist teaching is so special, so helpful to living. Though life has suffering, meditation, work both physical and spiritual and loving the neighbour and the community leads to happiness and enlightenment.

Nevertheless these ideals are seldom seen in these societies, especially when interacting with other outsiders.

In fact, in all religions we see the same basic highly laudable ideals. Yes all religions are very different but the intrinsic ideals are, in themselves, highly desirable and highly beneficial to all humans. They are not very effective however, they are not very good, and as a matter of fact they are by their nature, dangerous, murderous, controlling, and manipulative.

What has that got to do with God?

St. Augustine said, 'The biggest problem with God is the word God'. It has been so traduced, so manipulated, so sullied, and so tarnished as to render it unusable. The same can be said of Jesus Christ and all the other church and religion founders. They have been sullied by the actions of the men who came afterwards (and it was primarily men). We have made the mistake of thinking that the religion was the God; it is patently not.

Religions worship religion, not gods. We need to understand that we have free will. Inherent in that free will is our complete ability to reject or accept, and integrate or separate, as we wish. We need to learn to distinguish between unreality and reality. To distinguish between the actions and the manipulations of men and to become aware of what reality really is.

This understanding below may help you.

Belief is a verb, an action. It is a way of being. It is a way of accepting and understanding reality. God is not a being but being itself. He—and it is always depicted as he—is not some old man in the sky who judges and condemns. This is just the Christianization of the Greek god Zeus to Deus. God, or a power greater than us, is being itself, and the manifestation of that being is physical energy which converts to matter and spiritual energy, which converts to love.

We are free to do whatever we like. Yes, we are programmed by our society; yes, we are programmed and controlled. It is our job to see outside that programming and control, and to seek reality.

ENERGY

When we begin to understand, we can see and realize that we are made up of energy. Our whole body is composed of energy. Each atom, each cell, each part of us is made of billions of tiny parts of energy that integrate into each other to form us as humans. This is the same for every other living creature, inanimate object, and all the universe that we can see and that we can experience with our consciousness.

Science has shown that the universe originated with the big bang, basically an expansion of space and energy from a singularity. This energy coalesced over time into matter. All matter that exists originates from this point. Fundamentally, energy and matter (mass) are interchangeable. Matter and energy are different forms of the same thing. This is what we all consist of. The fact that matter and energy are the same, just in a different form is all we need to understand right now. We do not need to get overcomplicated about this. If you wish to understand this in a much more comprehensive and detailed way, then I will have a book on this subject shortly, called *A Power Greater than Yourself*.

We are made up of energy; everything around us is made up of energy. Energy is positive and negative. The whole universe and everything we can see, hear, feel, and touch is made of energy. Light itself is a form of energy. Observing this, we can definitely say that there exists 'a power greater than ourselves' in a physical and also an empirical sense.

This is how we can cognitively understand a power greater than ourselves from a scientific understanding. We do not need to understand it any more than this for the time being.

However, there are other ways of understanding, of knowing which are equally as important as cognitive understanding because cognitive understanding can only lead us so far.

We need to understand experiential knowing and understanding, and intuitive knowing and understanding. These are the sadly neglected understandings that we have forgotten about in our zeal for cognitive understanding.

We have all felt this, and we all know what I mean, in various different ways. Those of us who have been damaged, hurt, and traumatised know it in these ways, primarily through our anger, rage, hate, self-loathing, and disgust. We know that there are other ways to understand. We can understand through our experience. We can understand through our pain.

Learn to stop, to be silent, to look in a new way. This will take us a lot of time. See beyond the lies and manipulation that has been wrought upon us for the last twelve thousand years. You can understand things in manifold ways, not just through cognitive knowing and understanding. You can, by learning, begin to still and quieten your cognitive mind and try to experience experiential knowing, intuitive knowing. These are as important as cognitive knowing, and we have not been taught how to listen to them.

Try to experience the essence of what is around us, both in us as humans and in nature and the world. You do not have to do anything. It will reveal itself to you, and all you have to do is try to be still, to stop your shallow self-babbling, and look with your true self at the bigger picture. But you will resist; you do not want to do those things, because you have been programmed and taught that this is the wrong way.

You have been programmed to think the following:

You need somebody else to tell you how to think. You need your religion, you need your ideology, you need a way of thinking so that you do not have to do the work yourself. But in many cases, you have been so traumatized, so damaged, so hurt, and so destroyed that you had no choice but accept the way it was presented to you without any discernment. You were not capable of meaningful insight.

You do not have to descend so deeply. You have the power within you to stop at any time. At any time and place in your life, you can make a decision to learn to look with a 'bigger looking' and you will see.

You will experience 'looking' because it is not something that you can rationalize; it is something that you can only experience. You will experience a sense of profound peace and contentment, or what I like to call 'peace of mind'.

Then you will realize that this peace of mind is coming from somewhere. It is coming from you stilling your mind and plugging in to the energy of the universe, the essence. This is a power greater than yourself, and it will help you even if you do not understand it in a more intricate manner. You may not be able to see through the damage and trauma that life has wreaked upon you by either the perpetrators of religion or its practitioners. None of these people worship gods; they worship idols.

When you find this place, then you will see, and you will understand peace. This peace, which will only come fleetingly to you initially, is the beginning of the understanding of a power greater than yourself, and it is sufficient for you at the moment. It is all you need. You can plug into this power any time you choose, but to get to plug into it you will have to learn to remove all the detritus, programming, manipulation, pseudoscience, psychobabble, materialism, commercialism, hunger, and want that is around you and in you and see, that with a 'bigger seeing', you can know a 'bigger knowing'.

When we practice this over a period of time, we will meet resistance. Our cognitive brain rebels against us and says, 'This is just a mind game, this is mind manipulation, I am just fooling myself or 'I can't do it '. Well then that is fine and to be expected. It is not a mind game. You will see through experience, through experiential knowing, and you will know a new way, in a profound manner. You will find a new source of power greater than yourself, a new energy.

This is what love is. Love comes from the positive energy of the universe. It is our actions and the positivity of our actions that attract the positive energy/love of the universe to become a part of who we are.

You will learn to experience love because you will learn to love yourself. We have been taught to love ourselves as humans in all the wrong ways. We believe that we can buy love from the outside, but we cannot, it only brings negativity. We can discharge our negativity by learning to plug into the greater energy field which permeates the whole universe.

This is all we need to know and understand about this for the time being, because when people speak about gods and religions, they bring in ideologies as we have seen and now understood. With them comes their accompanying hates, clan membership, and sense of belonging. This inevitably leads to dualistic thinking, which is one of our biggest enemies to getting well. It is 'them', it is 'us', it is 'black', it is 'white'. Dualistic thinking served us well when we needed to make instant decisions, when we lived in small groups fifty thousand years ago. It does not serve us well in the twenty-first century. Dualistic thinking is a thing we need to learn to stop doing because it is consistently exclusionary.

The last part of this Act is most important. It is the most important because we learn several things. We learn that the only way to overcome hate and all its manifestations, addictions, and maladaptive behaviours is through the power of love. With the spiritual energy of love that pervades the universe, we can overcome even our basest and most primitive instincts. Our hates, our fears, our need for territory, our hatred of every other clan, and our basest nature.

To illustrate this, I will recount a piece of our early history, from long before we became sedentary, urbanized, and civilized. I have told you of our strongest instinct, our desire for territory. I have told you that we will do anything to preserve our territory. I have told you that we consider all outsiders as enemies encroaching on our territory. This is our base nature.

Twelve thousand years ago, Gobekli Tepe was built. Gobekli Tepe is in Turkey in the Middle East, where two continents meet. It is a large stone structure consisting of hundreds of massive pillars. Each pillar is approximately fifty tonnes in weight and richly decorated with both realistic and abstract anthropomorphic details as well as reliefs of wild animals and flowers. Each pillar is T-shaped, and they are set in a large circle over a twenty-acre site.

Extraordinarily, this incredible structure was built by nomadic peoples. Because of its enormous size, it required a great number of clans to work together to create it.

Thus, they set aside their ancient enmities and worked harmoniously, though they were mortal enemies.

How could this be possible? Not just the enormous amount of physical labor involved, and the huge numbers of people required over a sustained period of time. More importantly for us: how could they set aside their mutual hate to undertake this task?

In their gratitude, and because of their way of life in nature and their experiential knowledge, they created a communal space where they could interact with the power that was all around them and in them, in what they could see, and in what they could not see but intuit and experience on a daily basis. The power of the essence. The power of being and existence that they lived with every moment. They had no need for belief. They knew. They only had a need for acknowledgement of that which was real.

Therefore, they set aside millions of accumulated years of hate in gratitude for the power of love, the love that sustained them every day.

The enormous endeavor that they accomplished has come down to us, even today. This was the original 'Holy Mountain'. Subsequently, we have had pyramids and sacred high places, holy mountains, temples and cathedrals. Gobekli Tepe and the surrounding sites were our first mass communal celebration places.

If they could complete these herculean tasks physically and spiritually twelve thousand years ago, then surely, we can do it in the twenty-first century.

Surely, we can find the meaning of the power of being and love. Surely, we can set aside our hatreds and our clan and country identities and work together to reunite with the essence, the otherness, and save ourselves and our planet from spiritual and physical destruction. We can work to heal ourselves and our planet, in gratitude for what we have.

Now we have realized, 'There is a power greater than ourselves'.

ACT FOUR AXIOMS

YOU HAVE EVERYTHING YOU NEED
AT YOUR DISPOSAL TO BE HAPPY.
YOU JUST DON'T KNOW IT.

In our modern frenetic world, we are constantly bombarded with messaging, subtle and not so subtle, by all our media. The message is the same: if you own this product, if you have this job, if you belong to a particular group, or if you behave in such a fashion, you will be happy.

So, it is implicit in our culture that you need to do or buy something to be happy, and all attempts at happiness are to be sourced externally. Also implicit in this is the idea that you are born in an unhappy state, and you think therefore that your unhappiness is caused by not having certain things.

Therefore, we have been programmed to think that happiness and unhappiness are linked to what we achieve. They are not. You can be very successful, achieve everything your heart desires (wealth, money, fame, work, whatever) and still be incredibly unhappy. Equally, you can have nothing in the material sense and be extremely happy. Thus, the belief described above is simply not true.

Happiness reveals, it is free, it is uncaused, but you have been told the total opposite; you have been programmed from your earliest existence as a baby. Therefore, the corollary is true: what makes you unhappy are the very things that you do in order to try to make your-self happy.

You are not responsible; it is your programming. You are also susceptible to a constant barrage from a materialistic, commercial, shallow culture.

We need to understand this clearly. The materialistic, commercial modern world is like a successful drug dealer, and you are the drug addict. The more you take your drug, or in this case buy or behave in certain ways, the happier you will be. That is the message.

However, some of us know from direct experience that this is not the case. We took the drug or we behaved, we purchased, we bought for kicks or highs and it was great, but it did not last very long. We very swiftly descended to having to do this in order to live. We knew compulsion. We needed to take our drugs or behave maladaptively just to survive and to live with fears, to live with how we are on the inside. We used our drug or maladaptive behaviour as a panacea, but it became our Achilles heel. We became so predisposed to behave in this fashion that we genuinely did not realize that we were addicted.

This unease and inability to cope really began when we moved from small clans, became civilized and domesticated, and moved into and formed towns and cities for the first time. Ironically, another word for 'domesticate' is subjugate or subdue.

Therefore, we need to simplify so that we can help ourselves.

The three lies of which we are unaware, and thus unknowingly complicit in, are as follows:

1. That you are not happy
2. That you need to do something or buy something to be happy
3. If you don't do or buy something to be happy, you are a failure and are destined to be unhappy.

In reality we are doing everything backwards. In reality we are all acting on a series of false beliefs and ideologies, which are making us more and more unhappy. These false beliefs and ideologies are destroying us, our environment, and the planet we live on.

The premise is that we need to do something to make us happy when the opposite is the case. What makes you unhappy is that you feed the false self; you feed the outer shell self and you pile layers on top of yourself, making yourself unhappy. You are convinced that it is this that will make you happy, but it will not.

In a simple sense, in a materialistic world, the very rich become richer, and everyone else becomes more and more poor and miserable. Furthermore, it is becoming quite obvious that this is becoming exponentially worse and more prevalent in all societies in this world.

How can we deal with this? We have to stop and examine what it is that we want. What do we really want? Not the outer false self, but the self that we were born as. Why do we want it, and what is really going on? In other words, we need to get into reality, to look at the truth.

We are constantly bombarded with 'I can't be happy unless I have this'. But you can, you do not have to take drugs or stimulants or act in a maladaptive way. We are all trapped in the endless cycle of the drug addict. Buy more, spend more, get more because now it doesn't give us a high anymore, but we need it to survive: to survive the trauma, to survive the pain, to survive just basic living. Everywhere we are bombarded with this idea, this false belief. That this is the only way to get happy, and we are traumatized because we intuitively know this is not true. There is something wrong somewhere. There is a clash of our understanding mechanisms.

How can we get well? First of all we must stand back for a moment, just stop for a minute and look inwards. This is a difficult thing to do, and it will take time because we have been programmed over a long period of time to take our drugs.

The reality is that we have become predisposed to be unhappy in our minds; we are almost addicted from the get-go. This is the unreality of our reality. These three unexamined and readily accepted are making us unhappy in the first place.

We are prisoners of our programming, our mind, and our conditioning. It is not our fault. We have been programmed for twelve thousand years, since we first became subjugated in domesticity and civilization, and we have developed an addictive and habitual way of life. This is a fact: we are all craving. We crave the things we feel we must have, the very thing that is killing us, the drug of approval. It started when we were small babies, and it continues for most of our lives. Most people never see this, so they never get out of it.

This drug of approval and appreciation makes us see and behave the way we do, which is so bad for us, but we think it is good.

We need to know how we can help ourselves. We need to get well. How?

By learning to live in the present.

What does the idea of living in the present mean? Nowadays you hear a thousand versions depending on what drug they want you to buy. Nobody is sure, nobody actually defines it.

I will simplify it. I use it in relation to our addictive lifestyles and our maladaptive behaviours.

You are unable to live and to think about today, just today. So, stand back and imagine you are here on this day, this moment. It is difficult to do that because you are constantly thinking about things such as, 'What will happen tomorrow?', or 'if I could have this tomorrow', 'if I could buy this next week', 'if I could get this next year'. This is bound to make you unhappy.

The corollary of this is thinking about what you have not got because you did not get your desired partner, job, or whatever.

They are both just opposite sides of the same coin: you are resentful about the things that you did not get, and worrying about getting the things that you want in the future to fulfil your desires. But you are not living, you are not in the present. The only time you can act is now. Yes, of course you need to plan for the future, and yes, of course you need to be aware of the past, but you can only live in the present. As you learn to live in the present, the most amazing thing is that you start to get into reality. Living in the present really is stopping and realizing that there is a problem. The problem is not you; the problem is in you.

You will realize that there is truth in what I am saying that you are addicted, and you will realize that you have been programmed. That is not your fault, but you must do something about it.

Even shame and blame have become an industry (the blame industry). You see it everywhere. The consumer capitalistic industry is manipulating you even when you feel shame, so to ameliorate your sense of shame you need to continue to take your drug. Stop, do not think about what you need to do tomorrow to be happy.

It's the bridge between now and tomorrow, and the bridge between now and yesterday, that are causing you to be unhappy in the first place.

You have everything you need to be happy now if you learn a new way. A new way of living, a new way of seeing your true self in reality, not the false self. You need to look at this as if you are going to reprogram and upgrade a computer.

When you realize reality and admit that there are serious problems with you and with the world, you're already on the road to happiness. Understand that happiness is something that is not acquired; happiness is something that you already have, and you have it all the time.

Everything that you do is going to make you unhappy because you are confusing thrills, excitement, and pleasure, which are short term stimuli, with a deep-rooted happiness, which is there whether you feel good or bad. So, you become depressed. Depression and unhappiness are therefore caused by our inability to see the world as it really is, and inability to jettison our false beliefs and programming.

When we learn to live in the present and learn to start to abandon these beliefs, then we will come into the present knowing who we really are, and addiction and manipulation will have no power over us. Our mantra will be, "I will not think about tomorrow and my fixes, I will not think about yesterday and my failures, I am going to think about now. I am going to stay here in this space, because every time I think ahead, I think about my drugs, approval, appreciation, and the things I need to acquire to make me happy. If I stay in the present, happiness stays in me."

This is difficult initially because you are addicted, and like all addicted people you believe in false narratives and the fantasy world that you have created. I know more than most: I know that it is not our fault because we arrived here unknowingly, but it is our fault if we fail to act once we have seen the beginnings of the truth. The truth is that we can change, and that we can know happiness that we could only dream about.

Make the decision to be your authentic self instead of the approved, appreciated self. In other words, be your true self instead of your false self. The price of false beliefs is unhappiness.

There is no price for true beliefs because they are not beliefs; they are centered in certainty and reality.

The world has become a very unhappy place. It has become more and more unhappy, more vindictive, sadder, and more ideologically driven on false narratives, false beliefs, impending disasters.

You have everything you need to be happy if you just stand still and start to figure out what you need to do next to deprogram yourself. Realize that you are not, as the nihilists are constantly trying to tell you in this materialistic and consumer world, an accident; that you are not mere chance and that your existence makes no difference. It really is a mistaken view and bad science to coerce your understanding that you are a chance in a quantum universe and that there is no point, everything is pointless—this is what ideological science is telling us. Unless its not a mistake at all.

We now know and we are beginning to see what ideologies do; mostly, they have nothing to do with reality. Remember, ideologies worship themselves, not truth.

ACT FIVE AXIOMS

YOUR SUFFERING IS CAUSED BY
YOUR PROGRAMMING. THE KEY TO
UNLOCKING YOUR PROGRAMMING
IS KNOWLEDGE, UNDERSTANDING
AND AWARENESS.

We will examine this in three distinct sections.

We are being programmed from the minute we are born. We have been introduced to and attached to the drugs of approval and appreciation. In our families we learn behaviours and how to act and react in certain ways. We do not realize this is happening. Our programming is so ubiquitous that it occurs naturally. It is an organic process set in place over millions of years.

We do not live in an ideal world; we live in a real world, so nobody will react to everything properly. In the modern world we are all hypervigilant because we are manipulated by our programming. We need to acknowledge why this is so in order to change it. We can do that, and we must remember a very important point: our programming is not our fault. We do need to realize what our programming is, change it to the degree that is necessary, and acquire the tools that can assist us to make these changes.

All programming causes upset and real problems because it leads to unreality, and because of our programming we have come to expect things of ourselves. We judge ourselves; we blame ourselves; we judge others, we blame others. We learn things from our programming, like the false self, 'the little I', and the 'little thinking'. We learn hate, and we learn to belong to a subset group who think like us, look like us, and act like us. Therefore, we learn to hate all others, and we fear them because fear is endemic in our society. We need to see that it is of epidemic proportions.

We have a lack of respect for and acceptance of people who do not agree with us. Everything we learn through our programming, like inputs into a computer, is accepted by us as facts, as reality. Dualistic thinking is our problem; clan, group, country, religion, ethnicity, color, you get the picture. Therefore, group identity is so important to us: I am a Catholic, I am a Protestant, I am a Muslim, I am a republican, I am a loyalist, I am a communist.

But are you?

I am a climate activist, I am a survivor, I am a victim, you are not. You are not. I am virtuous, you are not. I am righteous, you are not. These are just attachments in your programming. Do not identify with them. Sit down and think about these things. You have received your interpretative and value skills from somebody else: your parents, your guardians, your religious or secular leaders, your schools, or your country. This input gives you the idea that you are what they say you are.

But you are not; this is somebody else telling you what you are, so this is not you. Your world view is programmed, the way you treat the world is programmed, and the way you react to the world is programmed. Sit with this idea and see. It is the first part of our actions.

You may be very upset because you feel that you do not measure up to the way you have been programmed. Therefore, you have constant anger, hate, and upset, and trauma and fear. Therefore, you become attached to things that do not matter, or worse, addicted to behaviours and ideologies that will kill you.

Sit and think about this, and you may feel confused or angry.

This is a perfectly reasonable reaction. Do not judge yourself. Though self-compassion may be beyond your capability at the moment, you are starting to see the real situation.

This programming is very insidious and dangerous, and is the cause of your suffering, because it has caused you to become addicted.

That is a fact. You might say, 'I don't drink, I don't take drugs, I don't watch porn or gamble, I don't behave badly, I am not coercively controlling, so how could this be the case?' But it is, you are addicted to the drugs of approval and appreciation.

The problem is that in our earlier years we only learn right or wrong, good or bad. We learn to be good or bad, and that often becomes the way that we seek approval and attention for the rest of our lives. We never actually learn to think laterally or learn to think outside the box or learn that there are consequences for our behaviours. We only learn to think in terms of dualistic behaviour, which has not served you or society at large in a positive way.

When we see the world only as black and white with no nuance from an early age, we can be wide open to manipulation. Either as a good child, who constantly feels the need to achieve, or as a bad child, who is involved in crime, These are opposite sides of the same coin.

Unfortunately for a child who has this very dualistic programming, by the time they are eleven or twelve years of age the elasticity of their brain has been manipulated to such a degree that they are addicted to the drug of approval and appreciation. Then they go out into the world seeking this drug.

'I want someone to love me, I want someone to give me something, I want people to see me as somebody good and important, I need attention. I want to win.' You don't; you are looking for approval, you only do it for approval. If you are only doing these things for approval, the problem is that you will never live in the present. You will always be thinking to the future, constantly seeking the things you have to do to be approved and appreciated.

Thus, you will never be happy in the present because you are constantly seeking goodness and happiness through approval and appreciation outside of yourself, and this can only lead to unhappiness.

The gap between 'I am now happy within myself' and 'I will be happy if I do this' is the cause of our unhappiness. Or in the case of the really traumatized person (although it does apply in some measure to everybody), they constantly look back with regret.

This is what happened to me. This is what I did. I thought, 'I am a failure, I am worthless, I am full of shame, I do not deserve to be happy.' Whether you are constantly living in the past, or constantly worrying about the future, the end result is unhappiness.

We must stop confusing happiness with excitement and thrills and short-term fixes. That is not reality. The reality is that we will never be happy today if we can only think about what we can have next week, next month, next year. When we accomplish things, when we get the degree, when we get the new car or the new house. These are only attachments; they will not make you happy. Conversely, if we constantly live in the past, always thinking of our failures, our shame, and our guilt, we become victims of our own minds, and it becomes impossible to live and be happy.

Added to this in the past ten years is the drug of social media and its manipulators, the corporate capitalist consumer culture providers. So now we have a new, legalized drug pusher with an even stronger drug. Our drug goes with us everywhere. It is always with us, and it gives us what we want. It fulfils all of our desires, via 'likes' on social media platforms. These social media platforms are becoming ever more addictive. They are getting stronger, with newer and more powerful technologies. Stronger drugs, stronger algorithms, stronger cravings. Since we constantly seek approval and appreciation, our need to belong and be liked is overwhelming.

As we have shown, over the past millions of years, we have developed an innate need to belong to a group/clan for survival. We have confused this with our modern way of behaving, which is our need to belong to a group for approval. We join hate groups online, or groups that we approve of and that approve of us, and we take on their views as facts. We become polarized or dualized because of this, and we do not think, since they do our thinking for us. So now we are doubly addicted, and we wonder why we are unhappy.

The consensus world view is that we are the happiest, richest, most content generation that has ever existed. If this is the case, why are we so unhappy and broken as a society?

We will be happy when we learn to deprogram ourselves. We will never be happy until we start learning and understanding our real needs, a critical one of which is deprogramming. This is made more difficult by the fact that we are in a drugged state, so we cannot think rationally. You are also in a drugged state and cannot think rationally, and so is everybody else.

I will repeat the following mantra throughout these Acts in the certain knowledge that, like me, you need to see it over and over again to really see it. To hear it. To understand it.

All our lives we have sought something that is not good for us. We are, unwittingly, constantly manipulated. We have to learn to see for ourselves that we are being controlled. He, she, it controls you. You will do anything for your drug, your fix. You will behave in any way you have to in order to get your fix. If you don't get what you think you need, you are capable of killing yourself. I know this from a personal perspective. I sold my soul, I destroyed my life, in my constant chase for this drug of approval.

We have to learn to live in a different way, both individually and as a society, or society will cease to exist because it cannot continue to function in the way it has evolved.

We know there is something wrong. Though we may be unaware of it cognitively, we feel it in our gut. We feel it intuitively; we know, deep down we know that there is something badly wrong. We feel disempowered and unable to do anything about it.

How do we deal with our sense of unease and foreboding?

Understand and see. See your programming which has led you to your drug of approval and appreciation. It is inherent in you, and unless you were brought up in the most extraordinary circumstances, with the most extraordinary people, you will struggle all day every day for the rest of your life.

In many ways, we have not changed one single bit in fourteen thousand years. We are still Stone Age people with more advanced spears (technology). We have not evolved in any other way, and if we do not become aware and make the necessary changes, we will cease to exist.

The key to unlocking our programming is, first and foremost, to acquire the correct knowledge. We cannot delete our programming from an earlier age, but we can become aware and rewrite the faulty programming.

The necessary knowledge and understanding are contained in these Acts. It will take time to let the knowledge go through all the roadblocks in your brain and in your mind, and to resist fighting it because you do not want to believe it, even though you know it's true because it is reality.

You need this knowledge, so sit with it. When you have this knowledge and it starts to seep into you, intuitively, experientially, and then cognitively, you can start to develop understanding. You can only develop understanding if you have knowledge. Addiction and your programming will block you, so you must persist and give it the time required. If you give the knowledge time to seep in, that will lead to understanding, which will ultimately lead to awareness.

We are chained individuals; we are like slaves. We have to cast off the shackles that bind us. We are miserable because we are not free. We think freedom is something that is outside of us, but this is incorrect. Freedom is inside us. Real freedom is having the knowledge to do what you want with your true self. Freedom in its deepest sense is the unfettering of our mind and our brain from our programming.

Begin to reprogram your life. This will take time. Your old programming will never be gone; it is on your hard drive, and since you cannot get rid of your hard drive, you just have to learn to reprogram the one that you have.

It is important to remember that not everything on your hard drive is faulty. There is some very good and powerful information there that has been there for millions of years, so we do not jettison everything, but with awareness we learn to know the difference.

You can do great things and achieve all the things that you want to do, for all the right reasons. It is not that you will not have ambitions, but you will have ambitions for all the right reasons.

ACT SIX AXIOMS
TRAUMA IS PAIN CAUSED BY YOUR PERCEPTION OF CIRCUMSTANCES

This is a very important act to understand fully and properly. It is the first part of our deprogramming. It is the first part of our acquisition of knowledge and understanding.

TRAUMA

Trauma is defined as an emotional response to a terrible event. This can be something such as an accident, rape, violence, growing up in difficult circumstances, being in an abusive relationship, etc. Trauma can be the hurt that was perpetrated on us when we were bullied online, bullied in school, and bullied on social media, whether we were devalued as humans, cancelled, terrorized, or made to feel unworthy or helpless.

In my experience, trauma is the single biggest factor causing people to resort to active addiction, either through alcohol, drugs, or maladaptive behaviours. It is an attempt to self-medicate a pain that is deep within us. It defines our lives and can sometimes destroy it.

The problem with trauma is that sometimes it is very obvious and sometimes it is not. We may be objectively correct or we may be objectively incorrect in our perceptions. What do I mean by this?

'Trauma' is derived from the ancient Greek word 'trauma', and it has three meanings:

A 'wound'

A 'hurt'

A 'defeat'

Therefore, we can see that sometimes the cause of our trauma is obvious and a little bit more easily identified.

Sometimes the cause of our trauma is not so apparent. Sometimes, because of our programming, we inadvertently attribute the reason for our pain and trauma to the wrong event. We may personalize traumatic events that are, in effect, random in nature but have become deeply personal to us.

We can derive from the above the following key insight. The attribution or the misattribution, be it caused or uncaused, blamed or unblamed, is not the central issue. This will never get us to the central cause. In other words, the reason may not be the reason.Therefore it is incumbent upon us, over time, to discern between what we attribute or misattribute as our reasons for being traumatized.

Fundamentally this 'deep dive investigation' is necessary only so that we may help ourselves because it is not important in and of itself. It is a discovery journey and no more. The fact that we perceive trauma is the most fundamental thing. Therefore, we will only use tools to help us try to distinguish between clear cut causes of trauma and others that may not be quite so clear cut only so that we may decouple from whatever that is, because it is all real to us. The effect on us is the same irrespective of facts, causes, objectively true or false, imagined or fanciful feelings in us of trauma. If we perceive it then it is real to us.

Usually if we experience trauma, it is caused; there are very few examples of imagined sustained trauma. In my long experience of addiction, and in working with people in addiction, this is the singular problem we must first face. This is what we are trying to take away: the pain of trauma, and the pain in our heads and in our hearts.

The feeling of not being wanted, the feeling that nothing is ever right, that we are unlovable—these are self-perpetuating.

The more we go down this rabbit hole the worse it gets, and we confirm our worst expectations of ourselves.

'What is wrong with me?'

'Why am I like this?'

'Why do I feel so worthless?'

'I am so valueless, I should be punished, I am not good enough.' This is devaluation, this chronic lack of self-worth. The results are trauma. You could define trauma technically in whatever way you wish, but it is not what an external person or medical person will describe. They might be right; they might be wrong. It is your perception of trauma what you are feeling.

You can only discover this as I did, through years of arduous self-examination. That is what real trauma is. It is not necessary for everybody to do this; you can circumvent a lot of it. You do not have to become a self-medication addict. I have known people, including myself, who really devalued their trauma, that is how bad it is. I devalued my own trauma; I was not worth the energy in the first place. This could happen to anybody.

'God mustn't like me, my parents mustn't like me nobody likes me'. I will tell myself all of those reasons, but it does not take away from the fact that it's there. We feel beyond redemption. Even God, if he existed anyway, would never listen to someone as lowly as me. How did we get so badly hurt? How did the messaging become so warped? Well, we now have an idea of how this happened and why. We have begun to understand the nature of power and corruption, manipulation and fear. We are more empowered now, We know the origin and nature of addiction. Our warped and nihilistic thinking, and our trauma, can lead to many disorders, suicide, suicide attempts, drug abuse, alcohol abuse, and self-harm. Deeply corrosive feelings of shame and guilt can increase exponentially, and we can descend into a vicious spiral, where the only way out is by self-medicating.

So it is not the objectification of trauma (though that is important), it is your perception of it that matters more, because that colors your entire life. This is the thing that you must examine, because this is the thing that you need to change as it is tied into your programming.

We begin to feel the sense of unbalance and unease and then we balance this with feelings of happiness when we take our self-medication, be it chemical or behavioral. As time goes on, it is less and less effective and we need more and more of it. This is the road to disaster, unhappiness, and death. By the time we have hit rock bottom, we have probably destroyed our lives or come close to it.

We have hurt all of those close to us: our parents, wife, husband, life partner, children, friends, ourselves. Yet we cannot see it because we are in such pain and deluded by our addiction.

Our addiction, as I have said, is telling us that we need more and more, and we will do anything (and I know this from my own experience) to get it. We arrive in a hell on earth, and we live there every day. This is the blight beyond all redemption, the unending nightmare, because on the one hand we try to justify our behaviour by our perception of trauma, and on the other hand we act increasingly insane, trying to deal with the active addiction that is masking our trauma.

We are at the end of the road, and suicide for us is the ultimate survival. It does not obviously need to go as far as this for a lot of people. I am trying to accomplish two things: dealing with the person who is in hell because I have been there, and reaching out and speaking to the person who does not need to go that far.

Here now, reading exactly where you are, is the beginning of the road to recovery, the beginning of the road to deprogramming, and reprogramming started when we first interacted with these 48 Acts, and is now working more powerfully, in you.

We have become programmed to look at things a certain way, so our perceptions become a part of our programming and are reality for us. We can begin to see a chink of light, where until now everything has been all dark. This darkness, ignorance and lack of awareness has led us to do all sorts of things we are now ashamed of.

It is your perception of trauma that is your problem, caused by your programming and your circumstances. Now that you can begin to see this indicates that there is a way out.

How?

First of all, stop identifying.

Your trauma may be horrendous, or it may not. The problem is that you are now using it to justify behaviours which are equally traumatic, and even worse, you are doing them to yourself. You need to start changing your programming by learning to change your perceptions. What happened has happened; you cannot go back to the past. We cannot predict the future, nor do we want to live in the future, though we would hope for a better one.

We can begin to change today by changing our programming and realizing that we can change our perception of our trauma. We can turn it from being the horrendous thing it was, into something we can use to rejuvenate our lives. To give us hope that gets us back to living our real lives and not the false lives that we had unknowingly been living. The only way to get well is to get to know our true selves and accept ourselves as we are, full of shame and hurt and guilt, and subsequently change our programming.

Through this knowledge we can change our perception, and we can live in our true authentic selves instead of the outer shell constantly seeking approval and appreciation. Thus, we can get well. This is incredibly valuable knowledge.

It doesn't matter what people perceive as traumatic or not; one may see it as terrible, another maybe not so terrible. The reality is that you can change your perception of trauma.

Remember it is not your fault; it is your programming. Now, armed with this knowledge, you can begin to learn to live in the present. You can do this by dealing with all the shame, hurt, guilt, anger, and rage that you feel, and begin to learn how to take ownership of what is yours and let go of what is not yours. They are all the same, justified or unjustified.

This is knowledge. Stop and think.

ACT SEVEN AXIOMS

BAD THINKING, BAD FEELINGS,
TRAUMA AND PAIN, CAUSE
DAMAGING RESPONSES IN YOU,
LEADING YOU TO EVER GREATER
LIFE-CHANGING REACTION EVENTS,
PAIN AND SUFFERING.

We have just learned that perception of trauma is the key to starting our journey towards wellness, much more so than the actual trauma. Trauma and the perception of it are like twins, with the perception being vitally important, but this is not easily obvious to us. When we are in the depths of our unwellness (either addicted to chemicals or maladaptive behaviours, or depressed, or stuck in controlling coercive relationships, or in general just feeling lost and alone in a nihilistic world) we are ignorant; and this is almost like a typical illness, a silent illness as we do not know that it is there.

Therefore, your reactions are predicated upon the false assumption of self-belief. Therefore, you will get bad feelings, bad thinking, damaging feelings, and damaging thinking because nothing is evaluated through the filter of a proper prism, but through the prism of trauma and perception.

They never go away; they become normative and a part of us. We cannot distinguish our bad feelings and our bad thinking from our good feelings and thinking, so we label ourselves as incomplete, bad, and worthless. We have all of these negative feelings and thoughts, and our thinking becomes twisted.

These bad feelings and bad thoughts lead to destructive behaviours. In every single case where these bad thoughts and feelings are present in us, they lead to responses that are not good for us. We self-medicate; in other words, we become addicted to substances like alcohol or drugs, which momentarily take away the pain. All the people I have spoken to in this situation have all said the same thing.

When I ask, 'Why do you do this? Why do you behave this way?'

The answer is always the same: 'It takes me out of myself, it changes me, it takes me out of my mind, it changes the way I look at myself, temporarily. It changes the way I interact with people; it changes my view of myself and I do not feel so bad. I do not feel so bad in my mind. So, I am living in a fantasy world, completely removed from the reality I need to get back to.'

This fantasy world, this chasing the next kick on which we then lean in order to survive—we have to have it, and it leads us to all sorts of desperate situations. We will do anything; we will steal from people, we will hurt them in any way it takes, we will do all sorts of dreadful things to get our kick. We will prostitute our body and our soul. This becomes our hell. This is the place we need to get away from.

This thinking is not your fault. This extreme addictive behavior is not your fault even though you have been blamed your entire life. This is not your fault, but you have never heard a good word from anybody in years. You have been condemned, laughed at, ridiculed, minimized, cancelled, demeaned, and shamed. It is not your fault. It is the only natural response that you have.

If your life is so terrible and you believe it to be so terrible, and it is becoming worse and worse, obviously you are going to develop a maladaptive behaviour mode of action, work, sex, anything to take you away from yourself. It is obvious that this is going to have a hugely negative effect on your life.

The conclusion is that we do not have to go to skid row to find this out. In skid row it is obvious, except to some of the people that are there.

In a sense, those who have lost all can gain most, because we must learn to die; like the story of the grain of wheat that must die to itself in order to live, to produce. Somebody can have a wonderful home, a wonderful family, a wonderful job, and everything seems fine, yet they can be totally addicted as er have seen. We have to change. We have to die to our old life.

If the addiction is substance abuse, it will inevitably lead to family problems, problems with work, problems with money, and problems with the law. This always leads to loss. Loss of job, loss of family, loss of dignity, and eventually loss of everything you have. But the active unaware addict will continue to be addicted. All of these losses are immeasurable, and yet the addict will, in delusion, be totally blind to the terrible destruction and consequences that are apparent, and that everybody else can see.

However, to the addict this response is totally logical and sadly inevitable. The addict will eventually end up in prison, in psychiatric hospital, on the streets, or dead. There is no other way. Add into this many years of pain and suffering, not just for the addict but also for those around them. The addict will lose everything.

ACT EIGHT AXIOMS

ADDICTION AND MALADAPTIVE BEHAVIOURS ARE A RESPONSE TO TRAUMA AND PAIN.

In every case, addiction and maladaptive behaviours are a response to pain and trauma. Both lead us to become very unwell, with potentially calamitous consequences.

As I have said, we are programmed from our earliest childhood because we are addicted to the drugs of approval and appreciation. Therefore, when things go wrong and those drugs no longer work, we need new, stronger drugs, or we need to get out of reality. The best way to get out of reality is to take something or do something that makes us go into a world in which we feel that we can cope. Unfortunately, this is not reality but a fantasy world.

The most important thing to understand is that it is not your fault. You have been blamed, maligned, minimized, criticized (and all the other words) all your life, especially as you have become enmeshed in your addiction. Everybody blames you, and your response is to blame everybody else. This leads you further away from reality as you live in the madness of your addiction.

As I have pointed out, it is your programming that is responsible, and your addiction to the drugs of approval and appreciation. Your maladaptive responses to pain and trauma are a direct result of your programming. You are not responsible for that programming.

It is vitally essential that you understand this. Even though you feel so badly yourself, though you judge yourself so harshly, though others have treated you so harshly, though you feel such guilt and shame. You must realize that this is not your fault.

It is your programming and conditioning, and your increasingly dualistic thinking because we have been brought up in a dualistic world. A dualistic world is a world that sees everything in a frame of 'I'm right and you're wrong'; everything is black or white, there is only yes or no. In this world without nuance we cannot cope, so we are on the flight to fantasy land.

It now becomes your responsibility, knowing these things and having this information, to change your maladaptive behaviours. You can change your addiction because you know why you are doing it: to escape reality.

This is difficult as it may be the first time that you have really had to look at yourself and admit that maybe you are powerless over your own life. You are just like a leaf in the wind, blowing wherever the wind blows you, with no control, and the more you try to exert control the worse it gets. You are powerless over your life and your addiction.

It is vitally important to understand this Act because we must try to do a number of things to help us get well. We must try to acknowledge that we are powerless over where we are; we have to sit back and understand this.

We also must understand that it is not we who have led ourselves to where we are by direct action, even though this seems to obviously be the case since we have continued on this destructive path. It is our programming, our pre-programmed addictive setting, and in our case we have maxed out on it because we could not cope with reality.

You do not even have to accept that you are powerless if that is too hard an admission or journey of self-honesty at the moment, but just accept the possibility that this may be so. Accept that you may be powerless and that your life is in a mess, and it is not what you wanted or dreamed it would be.

Every single person on the planet is the same; the only difference is in how far you are to the right or the left of the spectrum of addiction. It is quite difficult to see this because you see through your perceptions and your dualistic way of thinking. It is a faulty computer; you have inaccurate information, a faulty computer, in your brain.

Therefore, it is logical that your perception of life is not accurate. The next thing that you must do is accept that your perceptions are inaccurate, and therefore that the conclusions that you derive from these perceptions are inaccurate. You believe you have all the things that life expects you to have and that you should be happy, but you are not.

In some cases, we confuse momentary pleasure or thrills for happiness, but if we are honest, we can see that they are very different things. If our lives have become more chaotic and catastrophic, we know that things are not going well, so we need to look at our perceptions.

Do you feel lonely, sad, overwhelmed, hopeless? And you would say that this is part of the natural order of the world, this is the human condition, and it is natural to feel sad. But these are perceptions that may not necessarily be correct. If you are feeling these things, there is something wrong.

If you are allowing your emotions or feelings to affect you, you are unwell. You need to think about this because happiness is not something that you acquire; happiness is something that you have, but you can spend your entire life looking to acquire it. It is not out there; it is inside you.

You can spend your entire life looking to assuage and make yourself feel better with new things, new toys, new job, or new relationships, but they will not make you happy; that feeling is temporary. Happiness is not out there; it is underneath all the stuff you have piled on top of it. Your programming is telling you the wrong things and giving you faulty information.

You will have to admit to yourself that you are unwell. You may say, 'I want to do good, I want to be a good person, I want to help others, I want to be kind to my family, I want to set up charities, I want to help everybody, I want to, I want to'. You are wrong, you are sick because you have objectified goodness as an object, and therefore you have made goodness an attachment.

It is not, it is part of your inner true self, you were born with it. Your addiction from an early age to the drugs of approval and appreciation has made you unhappy. Irrespective of how you perceive yourself, be it as a great academic, a great spiritual guru bringing money and good to the world, a great lawyer, a great musician, a great mother, father, son, or daughter, you are wrong. By objectifying these desires you have made them external. They are not external, they are internal; this is where we start making our mistakes, because of our perception.

We are also very new to this way of living. We have only been domesticated or civilized for the last twelve thousand years, which is a mere whisper in our existence. We have been told lies for millennia, and our programming has become increasingly faulty with the amount of malware in it. Furthermore, we believe our programming and propaganda. We see it enforced and enacted everywhere.

Move on.

The following three points constitute radical acceptance:

I will begin to accept that my life is unlivable, unmanageable, and unhappy.

Through no fault of my own, I have confused the difference between reality and suffering and made them different things. I don't know the difference, so I objectified goodness.

When I could not live up to my own expectations, addicted as I was, I became worse because life did not pan out as I had hoped and been led to believe it would.

I am not asking you to accept all of this; I am just asking you to accept the possibility that these things may be the case. This is all you have to do. I am not asking you to believe it, I am just asking you to look at it.

ACT NINE AXIOMS

BECOMING SUFFICIENTLY UNWELL
YOU WILL FEEL COMPELLED TO DO
SOMETHING ABOUT IT, BECAUSE
YOU HAVE BEGUN TO REALISE THAT
THE PROBLEM IS IN YOU.

Having arrived at Act Nine, you are not now the same person you were when you set out on Act One. This is because although you may be very unwell, and even though you may not believe yourself to be unwell, you are now examining the possibility. Becoming sufficiently unwell inevitably leads to the same outcome, whether you are aware of it or not: you are in trouble. Eventually you will realize that there is something radically wrong. You hit rock bottom, the end of your tether, the end of the line. You feel unable to continue.

When you reach this point only a number of outcomes are now possible. They are as follows.

You will continue as you are, things will become exponentially worse, and your life will end sadly in a prison, a psychiatric institution, or a general hospital.

Otherwise, you will end up just petering out of life through inaction caused by hopelessness. You may indeed eventually take the ultimate step, the final act of survival, by committing suicide.

You are different now, though, because you have a lot of information. This is the beginning of understanding. You still do not have to believe any of it. You still do not have to accept it as true, but already you are beginning to accept that what I am saying may be true, and deep down you know it is.

A period of extreme unwellness can be of a relatively short duration or, alternatively, can be an extremely protracted process. Remember you do have the choice to get out. You do not have to continue like this. You can now act rather than react. As we have learned, when you react you do lots of bad things, lots of wrong things, make lots of mistakes, and hurt many people. I know this because I too have hurt many people and have made many mistakes over the years myself.

You do not have to react that way. This programme will teach you that you can learn how to react in a reasonable, positive, affirming way that will immeasurably improve your life. Doing so will give you something that nobody and nothing in the world can give you, peace of mind and the ability to have happiness.

I am giving you choices. I am giving you a voice.

If you follow this programme, one of the core messages can be heard in one minute, though it may take you twenty years to grasp it. From this moment on, you can accept the following if you wish. Every day for the rest of your life you can be happy; nothing will ever worry you, nobody can ever hurt you, and you will have no worries about money, family, law, or any of the myriad things you constantly worry about.

These are the motivations for us to look at this message because up to now we have lived in a fantasy world and not in reality. By the time you reach this point, and if you feel compelled to act because what I have said has had an impact on you, you will come to realize that the problem is in you. It is not caused by you, but it is in you like a disease. It is a soul sickness, it is a moral sickness, it is a physical sickness, it is part of you.

You may be very wealthy, or impoverished, or physically homeless, but you will certainly now accept that you are spiritually homeless.

Once again it is not your fault, but now you will begin to realize (not through judgements by others, but by your own realization) that you have faults. You will learn to look at these and forgive them, because if you cannot forgive yourself you cannot forgive anybody else. What's more, you cannot live a life of joy and happiness until you accept yourself as you really are.

This is a huge step for you because you have logically worked out that the problem is caused by you, and now you can take back your voice and use your powerlessness to your advantage.

Thus, by giving everything away and saying, 'I actually do not feel powerless, I am utterly powerless over my life and my addictions', you have already started to turn your life around. So, you have changed your polarity, you have changed the energy, just like a magnet. You have changed the polarity from negative to positive with your mind. You have also begun to change your life, because you have now empowered yourself to begin the next step of the journey.

You may not know how to proceed yet, but you have taken the biggest step by accepting that the problem is in you. What does that imply? It implies that you are beginning to take responsibility for your own behaviours and will begin to examine them. You have looked at this program and said, 'Maybe there is something to this, maybe there is something that I can do.'

This is so effective, the fact that you have repolarized your own energy. You are made up of energy, and you have changed from a negative energy to the beginning of a positive energy. Though this will take time, it will have massive implications.

You must learn to discard your outer, false self. The self of hurts, harms, attachments, achievements, and desires. Then, begin to understand your inner self and who you were before any of these additions and programming ever happened to you. That is completely uncaused; that is, you.

The story is told in all the ancient religions and in early true Christianity that you must die to live. Again, our example: A grain of wheat may look wonderful, but it is only ever a grain of wheat. When the grain of wheat dies it produces new life; a stem, leaves, and hundreds of grains are produced from the death of the one grain.

This is you, this is your outer, false self-dying and your inner, true self starting to grow.

ACT TEN AXIOMS

YOU DECIDE TO ACT, AND TAKE
RESPONSIBILITY FOR YOUR OWN
LIFE. THIS WILL EMPOWER YOU AS
YOU REALISE THAT
POWERLESSNESS, BE IT OVER
PEOPLE, EVENTS OR SITUATIONS,
LEADS YOU PARADOXICALLY TO AN
ACCEPTANCE WHICH LEADS YOU
TO SELF-EMPOWERMENT AND
PEACE OF MIND.

Here is where we begin to get back our voice, should we wish to. We decide this is how we can learn to live again, to live anew, and not in the misery of the old way.

How do we do this?

In many ways this is the most fundamental act we have, because we decide to take responsibility for our own lives. This has huge connotations both for us and our way of understanding the world. We have always believed, quite erroneously, that we had either all control and power, or none, but we did not take responsibility for our own lives in any event. Everything was always someone else's fault, or everything was done by somebody else to us, and we were always the victim, always the bystander. We were always the passive people to whom things get done, or we act impulsively and mindlessly, but once again, it was never our fault; we were nonparticipants in our own lives.

When we decide to start taking responsibility, we give ourselves back a voice that we have not had for many years, maybe forever. We have been led on a road of sadness, unhappiness, addiction, relationship difficulties, and all the other things associated with our inability to grow in any meaningful sense toward self-actualisation.

When we stand and say, 'Okay, we will take responsibility', this is not something that we can do instantaneously, but the decision to start taking responsibility is a fundamental one that we have the power to make. Should we make that decision, our lives will be utterly transformed. It will paradoxically empower us to realize that we are powerless over many situations which we used to futilely try and control. We cannot be little gods of our own kingdoms because we cannot control people, events, or situations. However hard we try; it cannot be done.

When you realize that you really cannot have a controlling interest in the lives of other people, events, or situations, this is shocking. This concept or mistaken thinking was what led you to your present dilemma. This new realization is, however, also the way out. If you accept you are powerless over people, this acceptance, this radical acceptance that you cannot do anything about them, irrespective of how they hurt or control you, will lead you to your own self-empowerment and peace of mind.

You are not powerless over you. You can make changes. You can act.

Deciding to act can be like sowing a mustard seed. It may seem like a tiny thing, but the decision changes you because it begins the process of growth. It changes the parameter in the way you look at things and the way you look at situations in and of yourself. It changes how you decide things. You are no longer a voiceless victim.

The danger when you decide to act, initially, is that you want to do everything at once. This is all or nothing thinking: 'I want it all and I want it now'. We have made this mistake all our lives. We have to accept that this will be a long slow process, mitigated only by the fact that as we proceed along this journey, though we will have setbacks, we will start to feel better.

We will have to realize that it is not possible to proceed with too much haste, but we must proceed as expeditiously as is possible. We will learn a method which we will outline further on.

Up to now we either had no method, or a method of our own making, which led to our lives being in chaos.

What does wanting to act mean?

It means that we are willing to change or are prepared to take responsibility for where we are, and learn not to blame others, however righteous that blame may be. Blaming others will only lead to our destruction. The only person we can change is ourselves; we take responsibility for ourselves and our actions.

When we decide to act, we can end up feeling totally overwhelmed (this happened to me) and end up saying, 'This is impossible, I can't go through with this'. Therefore, we must go slowly. We might also decide to act but feel no motivation to do so. The situation of being overwhelmed and not being motivated is common, so you are not alone if you feel this. It is the price we pay for our pain, trauma, trauma bonding, and our lack of discernment and clear thinking. This is one of the consequences of our past.

We will learn to untangle these things. But remember that no matter how bad we feel, and no matter how difficult things appear or are, there is no situation bad enough that you cannot come back from it or make it better, if you work this programme.

It is also a mistake to think that you can make things just as they were before things started to go wrong in your own head and reality. In other words, 'Give me back my toys intact' will never happen. Or you may think that you will have the life of somebody else, somebody that you admire, but this will never happen. You will have to look much deeper, because this time, when you act, you will do so honestly. You will take responsibility for your own life and take back control. There are very few people who are totally in control of their own lives, and those who do think that way are often highly programmed, in denial, and certainly not in reality.

Those who have lost most, gain most.

Though this is apparently contradictory, those who are really struggling, those who are suicidal, and those who find it impossible to go
on living, in many ways have an advantage. This is because we have
met the many events that got us to where we are now. Sometimes
those of us who have lost the most gain more, because when we
begin to take responsibility for our own lives, we immediately
empower ourselves. We are no longer at the mercy of the vagaries of
life, and we realize that we cannot control anything or be controlled
by anything, we are just in reality.

Even the decision to take responsibility does not happen quickly.
It is something that you have to learn, little by little. Taking responsibility is like building a house; it takes time. This is because we have to
take time to understand what it is we are taking responsibility for.

Part of learning to take responsibility is endeavoring to take
responsibility for everything we have done in the past, irrespective of
the situations that influenced what we did. Whether we feel that we
did things out of good or bad intent, were coerced into doing them,
felt we had no other choice, or were drugged or out of our minds, we
must take responsibility. Fundamentally, irrespective of the situation,
it is we who did them. This may seem harsh to you, but if you can see
it, this very act of taking responsibility will be the paradoxical one
that will set you free from the blame, shame and fear that have
pervaded your life for so long. You will be a victim no more.

There are always permutations, combinations, mitigating circumstances, trauma, pain and an endless list of reasons, but in the end
whatever we have done we have done ourselves. If we go to this place
of truth, this new honesty, then we are beginning to move towards
reality.

We may not necessarily like taking responsibility, and it can seem
like too much of a load to carry; hence, we must not move too fast too
soon.

Too much too soon.

Often when we get a sniff of wellness for the first time, there is a tendency to want to run before we have learned to walk. Some of us want to take responsibility for all that has happened without taking the time to separate what is ours and what is others. This can cause an immediate overload, and we can often fall back into old patterns of behaviour very quickly. Thus we endeavor to develop discernment and compassion.

If you have had a lot of trauma and hurt, have been castigated, vilified, minimized and cancelled, or if you try to take responsibility and fix everything too quickly, you can often become that from which you are trying to run away.

You must take changes on slowly. You must take them on gradually, one heavy load at a time. You achieve balance by taking things one step at a time, and that empowers you to become well. This balance is achieved through your own self-reflection and gaining of knowledge and understanding.

When we embark on this journey, after a while we will realize one fact, one incontrovertible fact: We have to accept that the past is the past, and we cannot change it no matter how much we would like to go back and do so. This may seem obvious, but one of the biggest obstacles to us getting well is our total inability to leave the past behind.

The unresolved past will keep influencing the future.

We must understand that even though the past has an influence on the future, the future has not happened yet. This is very important and worth repeating: Although the past has an influence on the future, the future has not happened yet.

So yes, we may learn from the past; yes, we may be guided by the past; yes, we may be damaged by the past; but the past is behind us and should be left there. Things may very well turn out the way we suspect or fear they will, or they may not. Fundamentally there is nothing that you can do about either the past or the future.

Do you see this? You cannot change the past. The only thing you can change is the present, and the little things that you do, bit by bit, can change your life.

When you begin self-examination and reflection for the first time, it can be very difficult, as you are allowing yourself to express and feel emotions that you have suppressed for most of your life. You will feel anger, shame, hurt, and guilt, but do not be afraid of them.

I appreciate the following is very difficult to understand, but you must try. It is vital in your journey back to yourself. Yes, you can understand them cognitively with your brain and write them down, but I say go a step further and do something different: go back, relive, and feel each experience one at a time. Allow yourself to feel the experience in your stomach, not just think about it in your head.

Do not try to understand it cognitively but feel it with the intelligence of the feeling in your stomach; experience how it dissipates to a point where it will never have power over you again. Nothing will ever have power over you again. You will learn that your thoughts can change your feelings.

We have to learn to trust what we are feeling, and this is how we will trust it, by revisiting all the shameful, harmful, hurtful things we felt in the past. Cognitively we will take them out, sit down and feel them with our other intelligence, our other way of knowing, stomach knowing, gut knowing.

For many of us, it will be the first time in our lives that we do something like this. You will then see another, similar paradox, which is that you can only find peace by accepting your powerlessness.

That powerlessness, however, does not mean impotence. Powerlessness gives you all the tools to be very potent and to act decisively, because powerlessness means accepting that reality is real.

ACT ELEVEN AXIOMS

YOU HAVE COME TO THE
REALISATION THAT YOU CANNOT
CHANGE ANYBODY ELSE. YOU WILL
STOP RUMINATING AND LIVING IN
YOUR HEAD AND START LIVING IN
REALITY. NO LONGER WILL YOU
THINK ABOUT HOW THINGS
SHOULD BE, BUT WILL ACCEPT HOW
THINGS ARE IN REALITY.

This then is our next step towards wellness. You cannot change anybody else, and you have changed your life trying to do so. Trying to perform, act out, cajole, beg, plead. You cannot change anybody else, and this is the truth.

Congruent with this, you will stop ruminating in your head ; in other words, you will stop rehashing the past and what people did, what you did, your transgressions, or the wrongs that have been done to you. Endless recycling, endless repetition, endless madness, endless futile conjecture.

Furthermore, you will stop constantly projecting, 'What I am going to do tomorrow, next week, or next year'. You will stop endlessly living in a fantasy land, never having a chance of succeeding in any of your hopes and ambitions because you do not live in reality.

You currently live in your head. You need to get out of the endless loop in your head and learn to live in the present, in the now, where you can do something about it, in reality. No longer thinking about how things should be or could be, but just radically and spiritually accepting how things are.

This applies to any human, wherever you are on the continuum of addiction that I spoke about previously. One of the hardest things we have to realize as humans is that we cannot change anybody else. This is particularly true for us who feel damaged by or caught up in narcissistic, traumatic relationships, traumatic upbringings, or traumatic situations.

When we have pain and suffering, one of the first things we often think is, 'I have to change the other person's reactions or actions towards me, and if I can do that maybe they might like me, or feed me better, or love me'. This is unreality, and changing the other person is never going to happen. Accept the truth that you can never change anybody.

You do this because, apart from your programming, you have so little belief in yourself. You feel so undervalued that you undervalue yourself. You feel worthless and unacceptable, unlovable, cancelled and dismissed, because you have been dismissed, cancelled, minimized, and victimized by the world in varying ways all your life. And it gets worse: this is why you feel the depths of hopelessness. Even in your depths of despair, and although your programming is strong, you will still come back again to believing that you can change somebody else.

You need to break this cycle by reaffirming over and over again, like a mantra, 'I cannot change anybody but myself'.

In the depths of your despair, and with your programming running so strong in you, say 'stop'. The other cause of your confusion is your dualistic thinking. The black and white way of thinking —you still believe that you can change somebody else. You can't; this is merely dualistic thinking in action. 'I'm right, they are wrong'.

You have spent a lifetime on the drugs of approval, appreciation, acceptance and all the other drugs in our programming, so you find it almost impossible to accept what I am saying. Instead of cognitively trying to understand what I say, try to experience it. Try to use a different way of knowing, not cognitive but intuitive; thinking not with your brain, but by stilling your brain and seeing what comes up. You will then see that what I have said is true.

Once again, those who have suffered more recognize this truth more easily. The problem is that they lack the motivation or the wherewithal to do anything about it.

Because of their programming and the trauma inflicted on them, they know this worthlessness intimately. Yet addiction and false thinking caused all of their problems in the first place, so now we have to figure out how to remove this inertia, this procrastination and fear.

We can now extrapolate from all of this the reason why we want to change somebody else. The reason why we are unable to change the ongoing, illogical mistakes that we consistently make, the definition of madness.

Even though these mistakes have been pointed out to us thousands of times, and we have endlessly repeated them ourselves, we keep on making them. What is logical to others is not logical to us. So it is not cognitive, intellectual understanding alone, as this does not work on the programming that we were born into but intuitive, gut understanding that will break through the barriers of miscomprehension. Therefore, it becomes clear to us that if we cannot use a cognitive process, we must use another form of intelligence or understanding to get around this problem.

What we must use is intuitive feeling, experiential understanding. This can be a revelatory understanding for the very few fortunate enough to experience it. We are going to change this fact and make it possible for anyone honestly searching to experience transcendental understanding and meaning. This should be the real definition of spirituality. The wellness industry could really embrace and take on this simple definition and use it for the benefit of all.

We must understand what is going on in a cognitive sense. Then we must embrace it and relive it. Then we leave it where it is and move on. We now understand intuitively with a gut understanding. Then we move on and cease to identify with it any longer because we have been freed from it. Freed from the negative power of the past and it's dreadful hold over us. This is one of the areas where we can fully engage with the power in the universe to help us to re energise our thinking and through our newfound understanding of this power of love, change our negative energy to positive.

Therefore, you can say that the old way of thinking and being was a hardware problem, not a software problem. You can rationalize in your head forever, but that will never work on its own. You will begin to see that your own feelings of worthlessness have gotten you here through your programming, not any fault of yours. It is not your fault.

In many cases we have been blamed all our lives, so we have been locked up, put up, shut up, and treated like dirt. We have buried all of these feelings within us, further drugging ourselves on the incorrect assumption that we need approval and appreciation to function; the reality is that we don't. Unfortunately this was what the world offered us, so how can we possibly think of anything else?

You need to accept the truth. It is not that you are worthless, but that your programming has made you perceive that you are worthless.

Accepting where we are is learning to trust. We learn to trust, but not ourselves, because we are unable to do this. Instead, we learn to trust reality and the energy that powers everything in the universe. This is the ultimate acceptance, the ultimate trusting, the ultimate belief, and the ultimate letting go, because we trust in what is real.

We will come to see that we are not random acts of happenstance or quantum fluctuation but are part of the divine essence. The essence of being that is being itself. We will then come to see that we have a belonging. It is right and proper that we are here. In a sense, our very nature is a part of the nature of a power greater than ourselves and is worthy of absolution and recovery.

ACT TWELVE AXIOMS

YOU HAVE COME TO THE
REALISATION THAT IT IS YOU WHO
MUST CHANGE.

We need to realize that the valuelessness, the worthlessness, the self-loathing that we feel does not stem from ourselves but from our pain, our trauma and our programming. Then we can begin to see that there is a gap between our programming, our pain, and who we really are as people.

Now that we have decided to take responsibility to act and to start evaluating who we are, what we are, and what our place is in the world, we can ask ourselves a fundamental question:

Why do I experience this inhumane view of myself, and why do I feel like this?

You feel like this because you have been programmed to feel like this, because you have been brought up on the drug of approval and appreciation. Nothing you do will ever match up to the expectations that you have. The one exception is if you are a narcissist, in which case you have completely unrealistic views of the world and of yourself anyway.

All of us humans see that we never measure up to exactly what we had hoped we would be. We can only be the best that we can be, and many of us cannot tolerate being less. We adapt this binary way of looking at the world: 'I am either all right or all wrong, it is either all good or all bad, my way or the highway, right or wrong'. We have no nuance.

The first thing we must learn is that this is the realm of the false self, the hungry self. This is necessary for us as humans, as it helps us to strive for self-improvement, and to be the best we can be in our outer world.

However, when we become stuck on the false, external self, we can become very ill if we don't measure up to our often-unrealistic expectations of ourselves and the world around us. Our false selves are being constantly bombarded and programmed by the messages of mass media, and social media in particular. This causes us to become increasingly depressed, anxious, fearful, upset, and unsatisfied, which is beginning to have a detrimental effect on society.

Now that we have begun to see that this is the case, we can look for the real self, the true self, the inner self. This is the first self that we originally had on the day we were born. This is what we need to try to develop.

Now you can act and separate the false self from the true self, or the outer self from the inner self, whichever way you like to word it. You can now see the space between them and have come to the realization that you can change. Now you need to change, and grow, nurture, and develop the inner self, the inner life.

Thus, you are now empowered to change. You were never able to do so before because you did not understand your programming. You did not understand the true nature of your programming, or that you were addicted as a consequence. Furthermore, you also did not understand that everybody else is also addicted to this drug of approval and appreciation, and their only difference from you is in the severity of their addiction or their ignorance of it.

The consequence of this misunderstanding or ignorance is very severe. It is as follows: you have spent your entire life developing your outer false self at the expense of your inner self. Now you can see you were very unbalanced.

Getting 'IT'.

Most of us have never undertaken a self-examination like this before. A true examination, in which we look at the totality of our lives in an honest but compassionate way.

Irrespective of where you are on the human social spectrum, there are certain inescapable facts or realities. You may be a very successful professional on one end of this spectrum or equally some-body struggling to pay for the basic necessities of life on the other end of this spectrum.

If you have never conducted an honest self-examination, the consequences will be the same. Whether you see yourself as 'poorly educated' or 'highly educated', you may still have struggled with addictions and poor mental health. You may have been in and out of rehab, psychiatric hospitals, the justice system, or twelve-step programmes, and yet have never really examined yourself.

Addiction of any form is no respecter of social class of wealth and status.

You may have had a gilded life of fame, extraordinary achieve-ments, and public acclamation, but this will not protect you from the consequences of your programming in the midst of an increasingly tumultuous and hostile world. Yet again I say to you, the conse-quences of your programming and your 'unexamined life' will have the same ramifications. You may be just like most of us, trying to live and do the best you can in an increasingly humdrum or hostile world. I say to you that unless you honestly reflect and see, with a big seeing, you will be destined to remain in your sleepwalking life. To get well, you must carry out the actions you derive from the conclu-sions of your self-examination.

I have tried all of these endeavors many times, but none of them ever worked for me. I would hear the constant refrain from others who attended, willingly or unwillingly, 'I don't understand "it"'. People on an endless loop of incarcerations and rehab iterations, those who have been trying to get free all their lives, still say, 'I don't understand "it"', and the question is:

What is 'it'?

And I now say:

There is no 'it'.

By 'it', they mean freedom from addiction, pain and suffering, the freedom and the beauty of having 'peace of mind', therefore the 'it' is the magic ingredient. But there is no 'it', there is no magic ingredient. There is only reality. Everybody can get reality, and thus everybody can get free; therefore, everybody can get 'it'.

There is only reality. I had never been in reality, and I had never understood the language that people use, the sloganizing of sentences, the ideological definition of words like 'acceptance'. I had never really understood what they meant.

Now I can see that there is an outer self and an inner self, a false self and a true self. Getting 'it' is understanding that I can have true, meaningful power in powerlessness, life worth living, and joy beyond comprehension when I understand that I do not live for the outer, false life, but for the inner life. This may take me ten minutes, ten years, or fifty years, but I will never be content and have peace of mind until I get there, until I understand that I can have peace of mind and that 'it' is a way of deprogramming myself and realizing that I am an addict and that I can change.

Living in the present

People will say to you that you must 'live in the present' and that the key to living is 'living in the present', but you do not understand what that actually means. If you do not understand what 'living in the present' means, how can you do it? It is like trying to teach algebra to somebody that does not understand numbers; it is impossible.

It is impossible to 'live in the present' if we do not understand our past. The problem most of us have is that we tend to live in the past rather than try to understand it.

As I have said in previous Acts, constantly ruminating about the past and our transgressions, faults, and failings, what was wrought upon us, and what we wrought on others, brings us nothing but destruction, because it increases in time and decreases in empirical verification and correct appraisal.

Alternatively, living in the future is a fraught exercise as we bring to it all our faulty programming, maladaptive behaviours, and vindictive thinking from the past. So, we live in a never-never land, a fantasy land. That does not mean that we cannot plan for the future, that does not mean that we cannot be competitive, ambitious, desirous of great outcomes. Quite the reverse: we can achieve a thousand times more, a hundred thousand times more, when we understand this paradox of planning for the future but not living in the future.

Therefore, 'living in the present' is now, this minute, staying in this minute.

How do we achieve this?

To get to living in the present we must learn to breathe, and we must learn to concentrate only on what we are doing now. This takes practice because we have spent our lives doing the complete opposite, and indeed have been programmed to do so. You must practice this action of breathing every day.

Meditate, because you will see that your surface mind, your cognitive mind, will take hold straight away. Over time your 'gut thinking' will start to gain ascendancy. Then you will begin to live in the present and know peace.

We have seen that for thousands of years (indeed since we became civilized and domesticated), humans have been destroyed and manipulated by ideologies and religions of different types. We have been manipulated by men for their own ends, so we have been programmed. People blindly follow people, especially narcissistic people who give them simple, binary answers to the complexities of human existence.

Throughout the recorded history of our people the same refrain is heard and is always something like the following: 'This is the way and every other way is wrong', 'He is the way', 'He is the light', 'He is our leader', 'He is the master of all the universe', 'He is all-powerful', 'Only I have all the answers', 'Hate these people, for they are taking your jobs, your money', 'We are better than everyone else because we are the master race'. The mantras are all the same and serve the same purpose. They spread hate and fear.

I, however, say the opposite to you. I am saying to you, 'Do not do this'. Never do this. Do not listen to the siren song of hate. Do not fly with the fire of fear. Learn to recognize them. These demagogues and false leaders are the main beneficiaries of the way you have been programmed. Wake up and see.

You can say, 'Well, this goes against my Christian values' if you are a Christian, but no, think of what Jeremiah said: "They will not need teachers, for I (God) have planted all the knowledge they need within."

This knowledge is in your heart. You do not need preachers or gurus. This understanding is there if just look for it. We are not advanced enough to understand this yet, but resolving to see with a 'big seeing' is enough at the moment.

Equally I say to you, 'Do not follow me', because I am not holding myself up as an example. Take every sentence I say and examine it. Believe nothing I say but examine it and see how it might fit into your life. By doing this, you will see that you are in a position to begin to implement change at your own pace, in your own way.

Accept where you are now, not at some future date. You may plan for and hope for a better life and outcome and this is worthy and just. At the moment do not think about this too much or in too great a detail as it will divert you. You are not yet free from the darkness. Remember though that the darkness helps, because it is only in the darkness that you can see the light.

Despair and hopelessness are my companions.

Despair and hopelessness were my constant companions in life, and I felt that I deserved no better; they were all of me. But they are bad companions, and they lead to bad thoughts, self-destruction, and bad actions. When we see that, we can begin to change. It is possible, it is not slogans on a wall, in a book, or on a video. It is not somebody else telling you what to do, but it is you deciding for yourself. Deciding to take the slogans and examine them, feel them in your soul, in your gut, not in your head, not cognitively, but by gut/stomach thinking. You will never have to look back in fear again. It is this fear that has been driving us through all our lives. Some of us have lived a lifetime of fear, and therefore we act out of fear.

When we learn to take back our lives, we begin to change and all things become possible for us, because when we live in reality, we can have peace of mind.

ACT THIRTEEN AXIOMS

WORKING A PROGRAMME OF SELF-KNOWLEDGE AND SELF-EXAMINATION, YOU ACCEPT WHO YOU ARE, GOOD AND BAD.

S elf-knowledge and self-examination are essential for us to function and to live as authentic human beings. Self-knowledge takes a long time and self-examination is very slow and very difficult; the journey is difficult but the views are good. Travelling up the side of a mountain will give us a great view when we get out of the tree line.

We fundamentally do not want to look at ourselves because we are afraid of how we have failed our programming, and of seeing how addicted we are to the drugs of approval and appreciation. In other words, how bad we are. How bad we feel we are, the wrongs that we have done, the embarrassments, the failures, the shame. We don't really look at our achievements, although they may be minimal or great. We tend to look at our failures. We obsess about our mistakes and non-fulfillment.

Prudent, correct self-examination will lead us to judiciously appraise ourselves as we are. The other Acts have led us to this Act.

We are incapable of being our authentic selves and accepting ourselves as we are. We need to learn and accept our present flawed state. Only by accepting who we are, what we have done, our flaws and deeply accepting our dark side can we begin to change them.

Learning to assimilate and integrate all we are, good and bad, paradoxically enables us to begin to disempower our false outer self and start to empower our true inner self. The reason we find this acceptance tremendously difficult is, as I have said, because of our addiction to the drug of approval and appreciation. We feed our outer, false self. We spend our lives running away from who we really are, and we live our lives mechanically, robotically programmed, not really living at all. In other words, we do not live examined lives.

Our ability to self-reflect has been lost to us.

In many cases an ability to self-reflect in any meaningful way has been lost to us. So, therefore, working through this programme will open up a realistic door for you to be able to see that which has always been hidden to you before.

We call this a Way of Living

If you follow this programme, you will learn how to deprogram yourself and you will learn to see what is really inside of you. You will radically accept the reality of you, now today, be it good, bad, past or present, failures or triumphs. It is all part of the real you. You can change when you know and accept what to change. You will learn to understand the difference between lies and truth because you do not know.

How could we know?

We have learned a false version of truth, so we don't know what truth really is. Therefore, when we are faced with looking at the truth, we have always run away from it. We run away from our own truth, which is revealed at certain difficult times in our lives, when we are challenged to look inside of ourselves. This is because we are unable to handle it, because if we see ourselves as we really are, falling so short of our prejudged, aspirational, preprogrammed life full of approval and appreciation, that would destroy us.

However, what I am suggesting is that with this new way of life that we will follow, we can gradually gain self-knowledge through truthful self-examination. By doing this, we will have genuine authenticity. We will know who we are, who we really are. Not in the outer sense, the false sense, not in the body sense, but who we are in the real sense. Not in a construct, but in reality.

We are now, in Act Thirteen, beginning to regain our voice. We are starting to become powerful in our powerlessness. We have seen, through self-examination and reflection, that we are dangerous and capable of doing very destructive things. The difference is that now we will choose not to do them; but we know the danger is there, and we will remember that. We are not innocent, and this is a good thing because innocence is impotence. By integrating the dark and the bright, the good and the bad, the shadow and the light within our inner selves, we become our authentic selves. The authentic self is unambiguous in its ambiguity, non-dualistic in its duality, and neither black nor white, because we have, or are beginning to alloy every facet of ourselves together and to forge a new, stronger alloy than anything that was in us before.

ACT FOURTEEN AXIOMS

THEN YOU WILL WAKE UP AND
BECOME AWARE. BY BECOMING
AWARE YOU CAN SEE ALL THINGS
AS THEY REALLY ARE. SEE YOURSELF
AND YOUR RIGHT TO EXIST. YOU
WILL SEE THE NATURE OF ALL
THINGS.

This is a very comprehensive act. We have come a long way to get this far. We are beginning to experience what could be called an 'enlightenment' or non-dualistic way of looking at the world. It is a humble way of looking at the world. This new perspective promises with certainty that we will be able to face anything that is put in front of us with equanimity. We will fear nothing because we have accepted who we are, good and bad.

Having understood that we all create a false self, and that this is the part of us that strives, that achieves, and that we present to the world like a mask, our outer ego is now clear to us. We now know that this is also the part of us that will align with ideologies and clans, with people like us, who are the same color as us and have the same belief system as us. Identification, group belonging, and all of those things are necessary for our survival, but in our human development we must make a quantum leap over this dualistic way of thinking, into a non-dualistic way of thinking, and start to feed and understand the inner part of us.

However, we must understand our darkness. We will become aware when we have accepted what Carl Jung called our shadow, the darkness, our capacity for evil.

In many cases, this capacity for evil was buried because we had
been so programmed into thinking of innocence or non-responsibil-
ity. You must be 'innocent', you must be 'harmless. The problem with
this is that innocence is impotent. We must truly accept the dark side
of ourselves and try to integrate it into us. It does not mean that we
must like it, but we must accept it. It also gives us power. It empowers
us because we know what we are capable of.

Now we know we are no longer meek, innocent little people—
innocents, puppets, tools, leaves wandering in the winds of programming and powers. We know that deep down we are capable of traits
that we would not be proud of. We must know these things because
we have done them. We all have the capacity to belong among the
camp guards of Auschwitz.

We can see in our modern world that we are all gatekeepers, we
are all camp guards. This knowledge, knowing that we are capable
through our programming of incredible evil or inhumane acts, fore-
warns us, forearms us, and makes sure that we will not do evil just
because we are capable of it.

We were running like automatons.

Because we are addicted to the drugs of approval and appreciation
and because we are programmed, we are running unaware, like
automatons, on genetic, specific programming from which we have
not awakened. We are like somebody drugged out, zonked out,
bombed out. Barely aware, we see nothing, we ask nothing, we appreciate nothing. We don't see green as green. We don't see the sea or
the sky.

We don't live, we exist.

We don't live life as it should truly be lived. Very few of us do because
of the way we have been as a society for the past twelve or fourteen
thousand years. Before that, our programming helped us for millions
of years to live and live a life. Life in its present manifestation is detri-

mental to our very existence. This is because we moved from a nomadic way of life to a sedentary, programmed, civilized existence, and it is like a veneer that is imprisoning us.

The scientific community will point out, quite rightly, that this occurrence has us where we are now, successfully civilized and in a postindustrial, high-tech revolution. They will tell you that this is a good thing, but the opposite is the truth. We are trapped by our very programming, which worked on the savannah but does not work in Havana or on the steppes and forests but does not work in the streets and neighborhoods where we now live.

For us to deprogram and survive the oncoming onslaught of various threats of nuclear war, ideological and religious wars (which are the same thing), wars between superpowers, genetic warfare, pandemics, and continuing global warming, we must have a quantum shift, just as we had in the upper Paleolithic period fifty thousand years ago. This time, because of evolution and the inbuilt algorithmic nature of the universe, it must be a self-induced, self-willed quantum shift.

This needs to be our second quantum shift in order for us to survive cosmically, as a people and as individuals, with a place in which to exist. If we fail to achieve our quantum leap, we will all die because we have become savages, we have become ignorant, we have not evolved. We have evolved technologically, but in every other sense we have devolved. It is almost like our evolution is going on two tracks: one forward technologically, backwards socially.

Therefore, it is obvious to us now that we are completely unattuned to and out of balance with the earth and the universe we occupy. We are ignorant of what we are doing, and of our fate.

It is all about control.

In our modern society we try to control as much as we can. This type of control is causing us to become unaware that we are programmed. We need to be aware of our addiction to the drugs of approval and appreciation so that we can become well.

Our wellness is about letting go of the attachments of control, or about forcing governments and elites to stop controlling us in ways that are detrimental to our survival and the survival of our planet.

This may sound very mythical or exaggerated, but it is not. Therefore, realize that your life is not about you. That it is not the 'I', the selfish, false self 'I' that we need to develop, but instead we need to grow and nurture the inner 'I', the true self. Getting this, understanding this, ultimately will save you and will save the world.

When we become aware, it will lead us to accept reality as real and not as constructs of the world we live in. We will see that the ideologies, religions, belongings, politics, countries, and facades that we create are all in a sense a repository of evil. They are detrimental to us, and they are detrimental to our existence.

We have worshipped idols for centuries. We have never been in reality. When we are in awareness, we know that nothing really will bother us, because nothing will have the power to hurt us. To get there will take a quantum leap which I call the 'new post-technological *Homo sapiens* quantum leap'.

This does not mean that we lack ambition or that we lack the will to do things. It is just that we lose our possessiveness. For example, a man says to a woman, 'You are everything to me, you mean everything to me, I cannot imagine my life without you, I cannot live without you, you are my everything, I need you, I want you'.

You have been programmed throughout your evolution, throughout your life, and by your programming to think that this is love. Now having gotten this far, and reading this much, do you really think that this is love? Is this your perception of love? Does it sound like real love? 'I want to own you, I want to control you, I want to possess you, I want you for me'.

This is not love. Instead, this is possession; this is control. True love is about wanting the best for the other person regardless of how they identify themselves.

You can see where we really are. We must let go of this possessiveness. As I said, this is the road to true love because if we truly love somebody, we will want them to flower, we will want the very best for them. We will never put them in cages. We want them to fly, we want them to soar, we want them to do whatever they can to reach the best of their ability, and we are the wind beneath their wings.

Now you are being given a gift of incalculable value. I say to you that if you can see and understand the true definition of love, then you will finally be able to begin to love yourself.

If it is anything else, then it is not love. If you think it is love, then you are unaware; you are being controlled by your programming.

When you become aware you can say, 'I can love you and let you be you', but your programming tells you, 'I can love you but also make you the way I want you to be'. This is why we are so sick. This is one of the huge problems in the world. When we become aware, we see the difference, and we will not get trapped in that way of thinking; we will be set free.

By the dawning of awareness, in us, we can apply the same thinking and understanding to everything else. Truth and love are facets of the same thing, just like a diamond has many faces but is still one diamond. Everything that is not true is a lie, and we have lived under a lie for millennia. We must stop. We must stop in order to get well. The problem is scientifically demonstrable. We know, by understanding entropy, that nothing remains the same, but always increases. Similarly, everything gets worse unless we make efforts to make it better. So, our very inaction and inattention precipitates our destruction.

By becoming aware you will see, and when you can see, you can live. It will not just be about you anymore, and much more importantly, you will see that you are not alone.

ACT FIFTEEN AXIOMS
THROUGH KNOWLEDGE AND
AWARENESS, YOU WILL DISCERN
THAT THERE IS A POWER GREATER
THAN YOU.

As a consequence of understanding Act Fourteen, you will see with your newfound awareness, or the beginning of it, that you can experience the world as it really is. You can begin to experience the world as it really is for the very first time. That means that every day becomes like a miracle. Every day becomes worth living.

You will become enthused by just how wonderful the world and nature really are, because you have become aware, and by becoming aware you have become conscious of reality. Through the knowledge you have gained and the growing awareness within you, you will discern that there is a power greater than you. This becomes self-evident as your inner journey becomes more sure-footed and organic.

What is this power?

We are at Act Fourteen now. We have gained some understanding and insight. We will now begin to understand that a lot of our problems are the naming of what something is and what it is not. We must learn to discern reality and truth. We see with greater insight that what something or someone is called does not necessarily identify what it or they really are. As an example, consider the following. An apple can be called many other names identifying it more closely according to its variety, Golden Delicious or Cox's Pippin or equally it can be called an orange or a banana or a stone. Nevertheless, the true nature of the apple remains the same. The essence of an apple does not need a name. We can identify it from experience and its taste. It is all part of our naming culture, our identification of things; it is a uniquely human thing. The moment I hear words like God, religion, or ideology, my antennae go up straightaway, and because my experience of these things heretofore has been primarily negative, I immediately turn away.

Every form of religion and ideology that has ever existed has been regulated by men for the control of men and women, irrespective of its founding premise or doctrinal beliefs, or its inherent goodness. It has been made complicated, formulaic, and ritualized to fit in with and exploit our natural clan system.

It has been orchestrated to manipulate our inherent trusting nature, our need to belong, and our love of structure. Most of all, it has been used to control and manipulate people in a sedentary, civilized setting.

Therefore, you are bound to feel negativity or disgust at this juncture when you hear these words. You can now see that all your life you have been manipulated whether by priests, pastors, ideologues, socialists, Marxists, capitalists, bishops, politicians, etc. But now you are in a position to stop and to think and to separate pastors, demagogues and controllers from what they are trying to control, namely you. The essence and real meaning of God has nothing to do with it. They are manipulating frauds and either have a very warped understanding of God, or more sinisterly do not believe a word of what they say but use your credulity and superstition to control you. Fundamentally they are all idolaters. They have maligned and misused the word 'god' so many times for their own ends that they have destroyed our understanding of it through their wars over territory, possessions, greed, control, and people.

However, we are now able to 'See'. We know what the truth is and what is not. We are in reality. We are aware.

They have destroyed for us the very thing that is true. Through the use of elaborate rituals, programming, lies and manipulation we became addicted. Now we are becoming free.

Deep in your stomach thinking, stomach feeling and dawning intuition, you are now becoming aware of and reconnecting with the energy of the universe in a holistic way. The consequence of this is that you are beginning to recognize truth and love for what they are in reality.

The idea of a power greater than yourself is that you can understand the power of the force of the energy of the universe. That you can understand that there is a force of love which permeates the universe. When you have learned (as I hope you have begun) to think with your gut feeling, with your intuition instead of just cognitively thinking, then you will begin to 'See that this power is there. You will intuit its presence everywhere around and in you. You will be sure of this over time because you have experience of it. Remember this: the only thing that you can be sure of in the whole of existence is your own consciousness.

The only way that you can interact with the physical and spiritual worlds is with your consciousness. As you develop along this path, you will see that there are many levels of consciousness of which you were unaware. Your interaction with existence is unique. You are unique. Developing your consciousness will allow you discernment. This knowing with a big 'Knowing' will allow you to see the nature of truth, beauty, and love. Knowing the true nature of things, you can see that no lies or manipulations can ever have power over you again.

This is the most important thing you need to understand: **The energy of existence is your higher power.** That is fundamentally what it is; it is indisputable, it is palpable, it is real, and it is true. It is always there, and you can learn to plug in to it.

We who have been very sick know this better than anybody else. We have spent most of our lives pretending to accept or else rejecting anything transcendent or with a 'power greater than us'. Moreover, we further believed that even if a greater power was there, well, then it was at best indifferent in nature or more likely hostile to us. Being disappointed and manipulated, and living in a world of unreality and pain, conditioned us to be distrustful. Now we can see with a 'new seeing' that our suffering has brought us to a new, intuitive understanding.

Reality is experiencing existence as it really is.

This is another concept you need to understand: the energy of living is the energy of life. The energy of you, me, our solar system, galaxy, universe. It is very simple, it is energy, you can touch it, you can feel it, you can see it. Equally you can see and understand its interactions. You don't need interlocutors who have been put in place to explain it to you; you can do it yourself. You do not need people who will manipulate you, who will take your money, or who will force you to do things (such as going and killing people in some other land) for their own gain, ideologies, or idea of 'love your neighbor by killing them'.

All you will have to do is experience and feel. If you have gotten here, you will see and indeed know that this is true. Energy is vast and beyond comprehension. This energy encompasses us and can be utilized by us to help us to become well. At some stage I will produce a book on understanding the higher power, but at this stage this is all you need in order to understand. Keep it simple, keep it real.

ACT SIXTEEN AXIOMS

YOU WILL HAVE A GOD, NOT OF YOUR OWN IMAGE, BUT OF REALITY.

A ct Fifteen ends by telling us that the energy that permeates the universe is vast beyond comprehension. Furthermore, we have now come to the realization that this energy can be utilized by us in a positive way. This energy will help us. Therefore, this is a god not of our imagining or of our own creation, but of reality. We have come to know and to accept the totality and reality of a 'power greater than ourselves'. It is everywhere. All around us, within us, visible and invisible, everywhere.

The problematic thing, as we have seen, is the naming of this power and the negative images and connotations associated with it. This is not our fault. It is caused by our programming. So, if we wish to ascribe blame, then it is with the priests, pastors, imams, and others who have used religion for millennia to control us, telling us they knew exactly what this power wanted from us. In the process, they led us to where we are now, at a crisis point where we believe literally nothing or nobody. We don't believe science, we don't believe empirical evidence, we believe nothing. We actively believe in disbelief; we are the great unbelievers. Conspiracy theories abound.

Therefore, it is now our time to make a quantum leap beyond our technologically advanced civilization to an emotionally and spiritually advanced one. If we fail to do so then the consequences are fatal for us as individuals, us as a species, and for the world. It will signal our utter demise.

The constructs and the images in our perceptions of a white Jesus, a black Jesus, a Christian Jesus, a Hindu deity, Muslim ideology, Buddhist ideology, capitalist ideology, communist ideology, are all just that. They are constructs. They are concepts. Similarly, a dollar, a euro, or any other currency is exactly the same thing. A false construct. A false belief. These are all the false gods that you have in your head, whether you created them or somebody else created them for you. They are all false gods. We have been idolaters for most of our sedentary existence.

There is only one real god: reality, existence in reality.

You can come to this conclusion not because it is a conclusion, not even because it is a fact (although it is an inescapable fact) but because it is reality.

In working this programme, you do not need to complicate this Act. As I said, I will be producing a book specifically on this subject.

Keep it simple. Keep the god of our understanding in reality, which will help us; we will learn to tap into it just as you can plug a light bulb into an electric socket and get power, because we are all part of the one energy field of the universe.

You will have god then, not of your own image or anybody else's image, but of the reality of existence. Being is the manifestation of essence. Essence is the cosmic universal realization of the power that underpins all that is and is not. From our simple point of view it is the power of love that permeates the universe. It is real and we can learn to engage with this power in a meaningful way. We do not have to believe in anything we cannot feel or understand. We do not have to adhere to dogma. We will not be under the sway of false teachers. Instead, we will engage with reality and a power we can readily experience and know intimately. What we need to do is subsequently written in our hearts. We are free.

Your awareness will enlighten you on how to tap into this energy. You will tap in because the polarity will be in the right direction. It is your job to change the polarity, and to understand negativity and positivity and their equal place in the world. It is both very complex and very simple at the same time. When we are illuminated, we can see; we can see with all-seeing eyes and nothing will ever have power over us again.

Not even death will have any power over us, and we will know peace.

PART III

THE SIXTEEN FALSE BELIEFS

ACT ONE THE SIXTEEN FALSE BELIEFS

YOU CANNOT BE HAPPY WITHOUT THE THINGS THAT YOU ARE ATTACHED TO AND THAT YOU BELIEVE TO BE ALL-IMPORTANT.

FALSE

W hen you are born, you are born free and innocent. As a small baby and as a child you are introduced to drugs. They will become indispensable to you. You cannot live without them, and you will become a drug addict. These are the drugs of approval and appreciation. You will also be programmed into accepting that it is normal and acceptable to drug a small child. You believe that you can only be happy if you can get this drug of approval and appreciation and nothing else. Now you are an addict.

We live in a society that has rules and modes of behaviour developed over the past twelve thousand years as a method to keep control. This has been important for our evolution, but as a consequence we have become programmed into behaving in a certain, acceptable way, congruent with existence.

As we have evolved into our sedentary lifestyle, these drugs of approval and appreciation have become ever more important to us, and our dependency is now rapidly reaching a crisis point. Unfortunately, so many of our young are now in chronic addiction, be it social media, drugs, alcohol, or maladaptive behaviours. Chronic addiction pervades society and is becoming exponentially worse.

If you are attached to something, no matter what it is, you believe it makes you happy. So, you need a new house, a new partner, a new car, a new job, a new degree, a new sport, a new pursuit. You believe that getting these things will make you happy. But it will not make you happy. It gives you a fleeting thrill or a sense of excitement, but it does not make you happy.

Driven by our drug addiction of approval and appreciation.

This attachment, this drug, this need for approval and appreciation, and this need for things so that we can feel well or can look well in front of people, is the way that we have been programmed. Our lifestyles, our fame, our recognition, our cars, our houses, our partners, our social media likes, are all false beliefs. They are all driven by this drug of approval and appreciation, and our ideologies.

We know, if we reflect for a moment, that when we get the new object of our desire, we are very happy for a little while, but then we become bored and we don't think about it anymore. Instead, we think about the next new thing we can get, or the next thing that we can achieve and strive for. It is never about the thing we have; it is always about something else. Constantly striving for and achieving something else, we are not content with what we have now.

This means that you are always living somewhere else. You are living in the future and waiting for happiness to come because of something you will get. This is because of your false beliefs that when you get these things you will be happy. This causes you to live in the future and never in the present. You are dissociated from where you are now because you desire something else. Maybe you won't measure up to the expectations of yourself or those around you.

There is a constant striving, a constant need for perfection, for more belongings; or constantly needing to look like someone else, to be like someone else.

With the advent of social media and its pervasive nature, it is becoming even more obvious that the early childhood programming and the early childhood drug-giving is leading us to a chronic epidemic of drug addiction. You crave approval. You will never be happy with any attachments or desires, because they are impermanent. They are, in effect, just like a hit of your drug.

ACT TWO THE SIXTEEN FALSE BELIEFS

YOU BELIEVE HAPPINESS IS IN THE FUTURE: WHEN YOU GET A NEW HOUSE, CAREER OR RELATIONSHIP, FAME OR WEALTH.

FALSE

You can see that Act One and Act Two of the 'false beliefs' are intimately related. In one sense these two Acts could be combined in that they are about possessiveness, possessions, and attachments which are linked to your drug of approval. However, we must understand the importance of isolating and identifying the problem of living in the future.

If I strive for something, I will never have it. It is an endless journey, the journey of a thousand moons, and every horizon brings another moon that I will never reach. If I live this way, I can never be happy. I can only be happy by realising that I was born happy, and the things that I attach myself to make me unhappy.

You are always unhappy.

You are always unhappy, full of anxiety, full of fear, constantly waiting for somebody or something to come and make you happy, but that might never happen. You may say to your partner, 'You mean the world to me, I cannot imagine living my life without you, you are my life, I am nothing without you'.

These are just cliches, and they are all false beliefs. First of all, before you met that person you were OK. Secondly, you believe that this is love. This is not love; you really just want to possess them. This is another attachment.

Do not possess anybody, and do not live in the future. If you really love them, then your feelings will have nothing to do with possession. You will want them to be the best that they can be without any payback to you. There will be no imperatives that they must do something to make you feel better. If this is the case, you can see how this will lead into narcissism, coercive control and manipulation, because you are now protecting your drug supply, your supply of approval: 'You need to be grateful to me'.

For any drug addict, the most important thing in their life is the protection of their drug and its supply. If the main source of your drug is a relationship of whatever form, you will do anything you can to control it and to make sure that you get it. You will stop at nothing; nothing is beyond the bounds of acceptability for you to seek approval and attachment in the future world.

It is a false belief to think that you need people to return something to you in order for you to love them.

You must say, 'I love you, but I love you without attachment and possessiveness, and therefore I want you to be the best that you can be, and I am here to help you.

'I must make this not about myself. I will not hold you back because of my insecurity, and therefore if you are not an attachment I will never feel insecure. I accept you as you are.'

It is real love to help somebody to be the best that they can be, and not to profoundly believe that you must control somebody in order to make yourself happy.

ACT THREE THE SIXTEEN FALSE BELIEFS

YOU FEEL ANGER, RESENTMENT, FEAR, DISAPPOINTMENT, AND SHAME, AND THESE JUSTIFY YOUR BEHAVIOURS. YOU ARE YOUR FEELINGS.

FALSE

We all feel angry, resentful and disappointed. It is part of the human condition. However, when we constantly ruminate and identify with these negative feelings we take them to a higher, more intimate level. They then become attachments which will ultimately destroy us. By constantly identifying with these insidious emotions and feelings, we give them power over us. The saddest part of this whole way of bad thinking is that we do not realize that we are doing it. We are reinforcing our negativity. We are completely unaware of what we are doing.

'I feel resentful because I did not get the job, or the car, or the house, or the right partner, and my life has not worked out the way it should have worked. I feel angry, resentful because I feel I am stuck in a rut or my life has become meaningless. I have failed and I have not measured up. I feel fearful. I feel an impending sense of doom that is always present in me. I feel a great sense of shame and disappointment'.

But as you can see from the previous Acts, these are merely reflections of the drug you have been taking, the drug of approval and appreciation. This resentment and anger at yourself and the world around you, these self-inflicted feelings—why do you feel these things to this degree?

When we have feelings which are negative or overwhelming, then we use them to justify our behaviours. The resentments that we feel are without a doubt the reason why we either abuse substances or behave in a maladaptive way.

I cannot stress this enough. These resentments are your enemy. It does not matter whether you have wronged or been wronged, the consequences are the same for you.

Our maladaptive behaviours become, over time, more and more present in us. It becomes a vicious cycle: anger and resentment fuel the addiction, which fuels the anger and resentment, which fuel the addiction.

As we continue on our voyage of self-reflection and self-discovery, we will now be able to stand back and become aware that we are full of these resentments and attachments and see just what they are doing to us and how they are destroying our lives. Only then can we do something about them. We can either ameliorate our behaviour or disavow ourselves from this type of behaviour.

We will learn eventually to respond instead of react. It takes a very long time to allow yourself to really understand what it is like to feel anger, to identify the emotion, to identify the resentment. When you can do that, ask yourself why you feel these things and establish the real reasons why. Some of them we will not like.

I have not measured up.

I did not get the partner I wanted.

I did not get the money or the job.

I did not become famous.

I did not reach my own expectations of myself.

I did not achieve; I did not make the cut.

I do not like the body I was born in. I do not identify with my gender nor do I like my skin color. I feel unattractive and unlikeable.

I should not have had to suffer the childhood pain, trauma, and abuse that I did. It was not my fault. Why did it happen to me?

I should not have been born into these circumstances. I should not have been born disabled either physically, emotionally or intellectually.

I should not have had to suffer years of coercive controlling abuse, nor should I have had losses, deaths and suffering inflicted on me by other circumstances.

I should not have been born a bad person.

Some or all of the above may or may not be the case. However, what is definitely true is that your perception is your reality when you are in ignorance and unaware, just as we discussed in the Axioms, and therefore they are definitely true for you.

We learned, as we travelled on our journey through these Acts however, that perception is not reality. We know where this comes from, because we have learned, and we are beginning to see with a bigger 'seeing'. The penny is beginning to drop.

These false perceptions and beliefs are the fuel and the origin of the drugs that you have been given. You are basing your thinking on a false premise which has now been revealed. This is becoming clearer to you as you understand. You see that all your resentments are invidious in their very nature because they are not really true. These resentments are insidious and grow more powerful as we feed them by constantly thinking and ruminating about them. However you have learned from this programme so far that they are only true in your programming and in your drugs, and are not grounded in reality.

When you become aware, you will also know that you are only human. There will be times when you act out of stupidity or unawareness, but it will not be to the same degree as before.

Through improving your sense of 'seeing' and your awareness, over time, you will see these imposters for what they really are. These imposters are resentments you absolutely cannot afford. They are the cause of your unhappiness. They are the cause of all your problems. To become well and free you will learn to drop them and to cease to identify with them.

Shame, guilt and fear

In a sense, anger, resentment, and disappointment are readily identifiable, and we can name them.

However, when we come to the more insidious resentments and attachments, these are more difficult to deal with. These are shame, guilt and fear.

Most of us have done things that we are ashamed of. Most of us have done things that we feel guilty about. Most of us feel fear, either of the consequences of our actions in the past, or the shame associated with them. We feel an overwhelming guilt and regret for what happened, and thus we are constantly trapped in the past. There is an unending sinking feeling in the pit of our stomach which we call a nameless fear. We can have shame, guilt and fear and not even realize it. We are fearful, always fearful of an impending crisis which is always in our minds and in the future, but never in reality.

We live in this fantasy world. We imagine all sorts of scenarios that never happen, and we live in a world of constant chaos. We feel shame, guilt and fear associated with our failed attempt at living. Therefore, we can justify anything.

The inevitable consequences of these false beliefs are catastrophic. We can no longer live with or accept ourselves. Our only recourse is to get out of our heads metaphorically. This we do because it is our only option; we can see no other way to survive. We continue abusing substances or behaviours because of our resentments and false beliefs.

We need to get away from life. We can't bear living. In many cases our last tool of survival will be to remove ourselves permanently. We need to run away from the constant turmoil and the movie in our minds.

Therefore, when you are on this drug, drugs, or maladaptive behaviours, in the short term you can avoid fear, guilt and shame. It is like a magic pill, and this justifies your behaviour. 'I had to do it, it is the only way I could stay calm and sane to block out my reality'. This is completely understandable; it is false, but it is completely logical in that moment and time.

When we are mired down on this road, it never stops, it never gets better, it never improves, but it always exponentially increases in chaos, dysregulation and disruption. At least if we can stop, look at our attachments which are causing us to do this, and try to understand them, we will have no justification for our behaviour. These false beliefs are not reasons, they are not justifications, they are merely consequences.

Therefore, it is incumbent on you to ask, 'Do I want to get well or not?', and it is a perfectly rational response to say, 'No, I want to keep blocking things out'. The consequences of the latter are very straightforward. They inevitably lead to insanity or death in almost every case. If we do not want this to happen to us, then the only answer is to follow these Acts. These Acts offer a comprehensive path forward based on absolute truth and reality.

The reality of understanding why do we feel shame? Why do we feel this awful fear, guilt and shame all of the time? In doing full and honest examination of our shame and our guilt we can begin to understand why we justify our behaviours, and only then can we begin to change them.

We are not our feelings.

You are not your feelings.

I am not my feelings.

ACT FOUR THE SIXTEEN FALSE BELIEFS

YOU FEEL ANGER, DISAPPOINTMENT, RESENTMENT, FEAR, SHAME, ETC., BECAUSE OF WHAT SOMEONE ELSE SAID OR DID TO YOU, AND THIS JUSTIFIES YOUR BEHAVIOUR.

FALSE

This is merely a more sophisticated version of Act Three. 'I act and behave in such a way because of what somebody else does or says'. This is the centrality of why we do things, because we react to what other people say or do, and why shouldn't we? Of course, we do; I know this from my own personal experience and from the very many I have spoken to. You will say things like:

'My husband or wife divorced me.'

'My wife had an affair.'

'My boss sacked me.'

'The bank robbed me.'

'He said this to me, she said that to me', and so on.

So you behave like this because you are in an ignorant state and you do not know any better. What else would you do? Of course you behave like this.

It is your programming

It is your programming that has led you to believe that your behaviour is justified in the first place and that the actions of others cause you to behave in such a way. So what else would you do, since your programming entitles you to behave this way. It is the nature of the condition, the nature of reality.

This is completely false.

We have just seen that the drug of approval is the fundamental reason why we react like this. Somebody else does not have power over you. Yes, they may have in a practical sense; they may do horrible things to you, they may kill you, they may threaten you, they may make your life miserable, but that still does not justify your behaviour. You want to run; you want to get out. Of course you want to get out—who wouldn't? Most people would. But this very act of running stops you from getting well and is allowing them to behave that way in the first place.

If the occurrence is a short-term threat, you will either be dead or not dead. You will be threatened or not threatened. It is much more dangerous if this is a long-term behaviour by someone you are close to who is coercively controlling you in a narcissistic fashion, and you feel powerless to stop them. This situation always gets worse. So the only recourse you have is to block it out of your mind and become that which they have said about you all along, that you are no good anyway. Then you prove it by acting out.

You do this in ignorance, because you are reacting instead of responding, and getting out of your mind to get away from the horror of your situation is the hardest part of this drug to kick. It is the hardest and the toughest because you want more than anything in the world to block it out instead of facing it, because it is never-ending.

The ultimate truth is that the shame that others make you feel, or the minimizations of what someone else has said and done, still do not justify your behaviour, and ultimately it is not good for you.

You need to get into these Acts and understand them. This is the crisis point, because now you have already begun to become aware of your behaviours and the consequences of your behaviours. If you do not get out of this cycle of behaviour as mentioned previously, you will be in this vicious cycle your entire life, and irrespective of what happens you will never know a minute's peace of mind.

You have to start to learn to drop all, anger, guilt, shame, and resentment. Only then can you be free.

Indisputably (and I know this myself) you might say this is a herculean, almost impossible task. No, it is not. It is very difficult when you are ignorant, but I believe that if I can do it, anybody can. It is singularly one of the most important Acts that set me free from my programming. I was finally able to understand that these things and these assumptions were false. I had been made to believe falsehoods to my own detriment, which destroyed my life until the day came that I could see that the drug of approval and appreciation and my programming were causing me to do these things. So, I needed to kick my habit and get into reality. Instead of reacting to what somebody else did, I needed to respond to them in a measured way, and **ACT.**

ACT FIVE THE SIXTEEN FALSE BELIEFS

IN ORDER TO CEASE YOUR MALADAPTIVE BEHAVIOURS AND ADDICTIONS, YOU MUST CONSTANTLY IDENTIFY WITH OTHERS WHO HAVE DONE SO, INSTEAD OF EMULATING WHAT THEY HAVE ACCOMPLISHED ON THEIR JOURNEY TO DATE.

FALSE

In order to cease your maladaptive behaviours and addictions, you must constantly identify with others who have done the same things as you. Many people who will be reading this, especially those involved in twelve step programs, rehab, and many other types of therapy programs, will readily identify with this experience. When they hear somebody else talking, recounting, sharing their experiences, they will often respond with statements like:

'I can identify with that person.'
'I can identify with how they are feeling.'
'I can identify with the last speaker.'

Of course you can, that is the whole point, but therefore you believe that this constant identification is good for you. This is not true; it is completely false. What is true is that the first time you hear someone else's story and it resonates in you, rapid feelings of identification will follow. For example, when somebody recounts, 'This is my story, this happened to me, then this, and I felt like this and I responded like this', you will immediately respond, 'I can identify with that'.

This is where we must reprogram ourselves, to change from constantly identifying with things to actually doing something about them. If we keep on identifying, we will never get around to changing anything.

For example, I see a dog. I have identified the dog; the dog is a German Shepherd. I do not have to go and look at the dog (or similar dogs) a hundred times and say each time, 'He is a German Shepherd'. I know what he is. Or I see a horse; I know it is a horse. I do not have to come back countless times to affirm it is a horse, because I know it is a horse.

As I have said, people who have been through rehab, twelve step programs, therapy, etc.. would be used to this identification in group therapy. However, everybody else should also be used to it because you see it on TV, you hear it on the radio, you read it in books. It is the same scenario in which you will immediately identify with someone. This, however, is wishful thinking in an imaginary world, so what have we done?

By constantly identifying we have immediately moved from reality, and we have gone back on our drug. Identifying is the same drug; it is the drug of approval and appreciation, and we can find approval in this wonderful world of make-believe. That is what it is—a make-believe world, a castle in the air—and it does not exist.

You can never be happy when you live this way because you are living in a fantasy world of the future. You must wake up.

I see these behaviours in others, you see these behaviours in others, and we identify with them. You need to change them within yourself. I change them within myself, not by constantly identifying them in others, but by changing them in me, and by understanding them and their manifestations within me.

This illuminates where I am, and thus I will be in a position to say, 'Okay, I can identify that within you, and here is how I can change that within me'.

By constantly doing that, I will no longer keep passively identifying with others, because each new identification will become a learning. The only place that I can effect change based upon what I identified with is within the world of reality.

Cease identifying with others and change within yourself.

ACT SIX THE SIXTEEN FALSE BELIEFS

YOU MUST CEASE YOUR MALADAPTIVE BEHAVIOURS AND ADDICTIONS ON THE INSTIGATION OF OTHERS.

FALSE

There are a whole plethora of therapies, rehabilitation programs and a vast number of wellness industries based on this sentence which is fundamentally false.

Take the example of the drug addict, the alcoholic, or the sex addict, and look at the concept called intervention.

Your family, your partner, your boss or whoever is close to you will say, 'You must stop'.

You will hear this as a constant refrain, and as you spiral further down the path of substance addiction you will hear it on a daily basis. You will hear other self-styled former addicts say, 'I stopped because of my husband, partner, wife, children, etc.' But you will not be successful in the long term if you stop addictions or behaviours because of the instigation of others.

The imprecations and pleadings then become ever more incessant. 'You must stop because you are hurting everybody. You are hurting your spouse, partner, you are hurting your family. You will lose your job (or you have lost your job), you are in hospital, you are in prison, you will lose your career, you will have no dignity left'.

However, the addict's thought process is faulty. As I have said repeatedly, the fundamental thought in the addict's head, all day every day, is 'I need to get my drug, I need to protect my drug'.

Because this is a reinforcing behaviour from something that you have learned in childhood, stopping or attempting to stop is only acquiesced to as a last resort to protect your addiction. To protect your drug. This is not understood, from my experience, by anybody unless you are, or have been, a chronic addict yourself.

Professionals in the sociomedical areas of substance and behavioral addiction treatments, though hugely well-intentioned, often fail to grasp this most elusive false belief. So, outside interventions, no matter how well-meaning, have the opposite effect as they just drive the addicted person even further into their addiction. Now the addict thinks everybody is against them, the world is against them, and that confirms their thought process which is, by its very nature, faulty anyway.

If we take for example the multi-addicted person. This is a person who has been programmed from birth like us all, but they are also addicted to a behaviour or a substance, or a combination of any forms of substances and behaviours. I believe that the second addiction is just a reinforcement. Thus, they are a confirmation of the earlier addiction, a way of getting away from the world and reality, pain, trauma, fear.

People will say, 'You must stop your behaviour'.

Both you and they believe that you will, but you won't. What they do not realize is that your behaviour, which to the outsider looks abnormal, has become your normal.

The abnormal becomes normal in addiction. This in turn can lead you to live in coercive, controlling, narcissistic relationships because you will accept anything just to belong and feel loved. You will accept and even welcome any form of abusive relationship if it enables you to protect your addiction.

You will also endure abuse in the workplace, in the home, and in so-called friendships because you think it is acceptable. You will debase yourself, you will lose your looks, your health, and eventually you will lose everything. Somebody else telling you to stop will not work; you must want it yourself.

The problem is that with your programming, false assumptions, and your early addiction to approval and appreciation, you believe that you are not worth anything. Therefore, you are prepared to take on the false belief that others can make or implore you to stop on face value, 'Oh, I will stop to please somebody else'. This is nonsense. You will pretend to stop to get people off your back. Period.

This is the reason why people stay addicted for years in the most appalling circumstances. Ruined lives, deaths, and suicides are based on these false assumptions, errors of thinking, and an industry that is making vast amounts of money out of other people's misery. Therefore you say, 'I can't do it, it is impossible, and anyway I am not worth it'.

The 'I can't do it' part may not be accurate, because everything you have done heretofore is based on false beliefs and false assumptions. However, I know that you can get well, and the only way to get well and to stay well is to follow this programme and begin the journey of acquiring knowledge and understanding. You do not have to be mainstream educated; it is self-explanatory.

When you begin to understand, you will see that the shame and guilt that you feel are not accurate; because everything you have done is not real in the first place, the shame and guilt cannot be real. They are not real to you, even though the events are true, and the consequences are very real to others. You have lived in unreality, so they are manifestations of your programming, but they are not you, and you are not defined by them. Yes, there are strong reasons why you should feel shame and guilt, but I am telling you it is not your fault.

You may have done terrible things, and you may have hurt people. You cannot do anything about what you have done in the past, but you have now learned to take responsibility for it. There may well be mitigating circumstances as to why you did these things, but fundamentally shame and guilt are corrosive emotions, and if you do not try and understand them you will keep repeating the same mistakes of the past, over and over again until they eventually kill you.

To get rid of them, you must take responsibility for your life and get into reality by following this programme and coming into awareness. When you come into awareness you will be able to say:

'Yes, I did that, but I was unaware. I did all those things, but I was unaware'.

'I did not know then what I know now'.

'I will never do those things now that I understand and have started to come into awareness and reality'.

'I will try as much as I can to make amends for the things that I have done, but at the end of the day, if I want to be well, I will have to realize that guilt and shame have to go'.

'I must look at the root cause of my feelings, because shame in particular can be very deep-rooted and corrosive'.

'In other words, I will learn to forgive myself, I will learn to love myself, I will learn to tap into the power of love in the universe'.

You must stop for yourself.

Reading the Acts so far, you have begun to grasp that you are worth redemption.

ACT SEVEN THE SIXTEEN FALSE BELIEFS

YOU WILL BE HAPPY IF YOU CHANGE OTHERS, OR IF THE PEOPLE CLOSEST TO YOU CHANGE.

FALSE

This is a very common idea which I will call a misconception or even a delusion. We must get rid of it.

'If only she would change.'

'If only he would change.'

'If only they would treat me differently.'

'If only they loved me.'

'If only this, if only that, if only, if'.

This delusion is a complete waste of time. It is a false assumption, a false belief. It is another one built on false programming. You cannot change others. You cannot even hope others will change, because that is living in a fantasy world called the 'improbable future' or more accurately the 'Impossible future'.

This is the worst possible place you could be. I have spent most of my life trying to change others, hoping other people will change. It never happened, it never worked. I eventually had to come to the realization that the only person that I could change was myself.

When I changed, other people changed around me, purely because of the changes I had instigated in myself.

ACT EIGHT THE SIXTEEN
FALSE BELIEFS

HAPPINESS IS IN THINGS, PEOPLE, POSSESSIONS, AND THE WORLD OUTSIDE.

FALSE

You may believe that happiness is an exterior thing, but that is not true. Or you may think that happiness is found, bought, achieved, purchased, worked for, or worked towards. All these ideas are your programming, Happiness is not found in external things; happiness is within.

You were born happy. Think about this. You were born happy. You chose to add things to your life, and these are the things that have made you unhappy. You did it because of your programming, your false perceptions, your drugs of approval and appreciation, and the ensuing assumptions. Please stand back and look at what I am saying.

Happiness is not excitement and momentary thrills.

We confuse two things because of our programming and our early experience of our drugs of approval. We confuse happiness with excitement. We confuse contentment with thrills. This confusion causes our unhappiness as we cannot tell these things apart due to our faulty programming.

All your possessions, all the things you have done and achieved will never make you happy. You don't even know what happiness is. In the mad pursuit for happiness, you become even more unhappy because of your false beliefs and programming.

You have to understand there is no happiness to be found in external things, merely thrills and excitement. These are just momentary and will inevitably lead you to seek more and more in an ever descending spiral. As with alcohol or an opiate, the desire for it starts off small, but after a while more is needed to produce the same effect, and more, and more. You become addicted to it, whatever it is. You need it to get more of this feeling, because you have confused thrills and excitement with happiness and contentment.

Other people cannot make you happy, no matter who they are. You view them as objects. You want them for what they do for you. Consequently, you do not want them for who they are. Therefore, whenever they do something that may displease you, you view it disproportionately. People, irrespective of who they are, can give you good feelings because they meet your expectations. You confuse this with love. When you leave people free and without qualification or expectation, only then can you love them. You can learn to love everybody, even your enemy. As a result, you will have no expectations of happiness from them, but find happiness in them. Nobody will ever upset you again.

ACT NINE THE SIXTEEN FALSE BELIEFS

IF I CHANGE EVERYTHING I HAVE, AND ACHIEVE EVERYTHING I WISH TO DO, I WILL BE HAPPY.

FALSE

This is one of the great untruths of the human condition, and we believe it implicitly. It drives us, it makes us succeed, and it is necessary for us to win, but it is also fundamentally flawed. I am not talking about ambition and desire to better the world, to achieve so that others may benefit. This has nothing to do with what I am talking about. I am talking about this idea: 'If I change everything I have, and achieve everything I wish to do, I will be happy'.

This is all about feeding the false, outer self. It is the false self that achieves all these things, owns all these things, possesses all these things, keeps all these things in control. This is the small self, the one that dies when you die.

Instead, you need to nurture and feed the inner self, the true self.

Consider these progressively more sophisticated examples of genuinely held false beliefs and actions:

'I give something to myself because it makes me happy, I do something for myself because it makes me happy' (fair enough).

'I give something to someone else because it makes me happy' (a little more sophisticated).

'I give everything away so that it appears I have done great things, but this is equally all about me, the false self'.

'I run and support worthy charities. I initiate new ventures so that I can be seen helping people and that makes me feel good'.

We can become delusional. It's all about others when it is really all about us. Why do we do this? Are we bad selfish people? No, of course we are not bad or selfish people. We are just operating and behaving according to our programming and our craving for our drugs of approval and appreciation.

One of the many things that advertising, social media, TV, magazines, cinema, books, etc. sell is the false belief that you will feel better if you get this, if you buy that, if you own this, do that. If you achieve and get to the top of your profession, excel in sport, art, music, or similar endeavors, and become famous, you will be happy. You won't; you are just feeding your drug of approval, which will never make you happy. If you do not believe me, ask anyone who has done so, and if they are honest with you, not one of them will tell you that it made them happy.

The giving is our recompense.

You may achieve anything you want, and you can do anything you want, not for happiness' sake, but because you feel that this is the right thing for you. Furthermore, you can do something for somebody else, or you can give to somebody else, for the sake of the inner you, not the outer shell. But if you do this solely to make you happy about yourself, then it is a complete waste of time.

Achieving our hearts desire.

We have it all. We have everything we ever dreamed of and more.

Does this make us happy? Well, that depends. If we have grown personally as we have achieved and when we arrive at where we wished to arrive mentally and spiritually integrated and with a highly developed knowledge of ourselves derived from strain, pain effort and suffering then yes, we will be content. We have learned gratitude. We have learned to be grateful for all the gifts and blessings we have had along the way. We are grateful for our growth, our relationships and all we have done, not in and of themselves but because we have brought joy and fulfilment to ourselves and others. We are especially grateful for our suffering since it has taught us all we know in every way. We have come to understand that life is not all about us.

However, if we achieve our hearts desire and more, much more, but we have not grown inside, mentally, and spiritually, then we will never know happiness. Though we own vast fortunes or control governments and countries we will never know peace. All we will ever know is momentary kicks and thrills and they do not last long. So, then we need more of the same drug or another fix somewhere else or anything to fill the emptiness in the pit of our stomach. The pit that can never be filled. The bottomless pit of emptiness. When we look with our newfound dawning of awareness, we see that there are many examples of this in plain sight.

In fact, I was a prime example of the need to achieve and to have possessions for all the wrong reasons myself. It was all about me, the little frightened insecure me. I could never have enough of appear to have enough. I wanted admiration, I wanted approval, I wanted appreciation.

It took me a very long time to learn that this was a road to no town. The rapacious hunger of my craving became a hunger so vast that in the end, nothing could assuage it.

As I lived, suffered, discovered, and put in place the programme that I am now setting out here, it was revealed to me that there was a much better way. A way to live without the pain of craving. A way to be free and enjoy life as it is in all its wonder and beauty.

ACT TEN THE SIXTEEN FALSE BELIEFS

WILL BE HAPPY. IF ALL MY DESIRES ARE FULFILLED AND ALL MY DREAMS COME TRUE, THEN I

FALSE

It is wonderful to have dreams of success and dreams of achievement, be they on a personal or professional level. To dream of having a great career or a great job. To have a great relationship, a good family, to be a good partner, parent, to be a decent person, to help others— these are wonderful things. We need these dreams to spur us on, but fulfilling all of these dreams will not make us happy unless we do them for the right reason.

We need to define happiness in this context. Happiness is not excitement and thrills, ecstasy, or jubilation, because all of these are momentary and illusory. They credit and maintain the outer, false self that we present to the world, but they are not us. To be able to enjoy the world, nature, and other people, and to participate in a meaningful way in our song of life, we need to learn a new definition of happiness. If we do this, we will grow our inner selves and we will live joyfully with peace and contentment, unafraid of the future.

In this form of happiness, we see the world and all around us like a great song. In this way of looking at the world, we hear the music and the rhythm and the words and the singer. Thus, the song is neither the words, the music, or the singer, but a living thing. Happiness is our ability to sing with the singer.

If all our dreams are about us, we need attention for ourselves, and everything is all about our selfish desires, our achievements for our own ends only. In that case, it is all about our ego, our power, our fame. These dreams will become our nightmares, because we will have achieved nothing except an empty shell, a false self-driven by ego. If we feed our inner self and desire to live harmoniously in the world so that others can benefit from our gifts, then our dreams are a wonderful thing. We must distinguish between the two motives.

There is also an insidious third part to this. When our dreams become fantasy dreams to take us away from the horror of the reality that we live in, this can be dangerous. We dream of somebody coming to save us. We dream of huge changes that will happen out of the blue, that something will happen that will change our terrible circumstances. Now we are in unreality; this is never good, this is disastrous. We must retreat from such dreams because they are not helpful dreams. They are fantasy dreams that just serve to take us away from reality like our drugs do. We need to stop these and get into reality.

If all my desires are fulfilled

Every time we desire something we are setting ourselves up for unhappiness because desire is possessiveness. Desire is a craving like that for a drug. Desire causes us to do anything we have to do in order to control other people and situations. It drives us to behave in appalling ways because our desires override our basic, decent humanity. Desire, like possessiveness, like shame, is a corrosive emotion, and it brings about our downfall.

Your desires can never be fulfilled.

Your desires can never be fulfilled. They are unending, so fulfillment is impossible; you end up in the realm of the pot-bellied monster, and the more you feed it the hungrier it gets. Your desires become boundless, and every day you must feed them more and more until eventually they become an addiction that can never be sated.

If my dreams come true but at enormous cost, they are valueless. Whereas if I have knowledge which leads me to some form of understanding and awareness, and I notice and understand my desires and dreams for what they really are, I will drop them.

I am aware of the dreams that I have, and the dreams that I can bring to fruition and to reality. I do not live in a fantasy world taking me away from reality, but in a dream towards reality.

Unfortunately for most of us, we do not want to live in reality; we want to live in fantasy dreams because we cannot handle reality. Therefore, drop desires, drop fantasy dreams which only feed the outer, false self, and get into reality.

ACT ELEVEN THE SIXTEEN FALSE BELIEFS

IF MY LOVE DEPENDS ON OTHERS, AND I CLING TO THEM AND CONTROL THEM IN A CAGE OF LOVE, I WILL BE HAPPY.

FALSE

If my love depends on others and I cling to them and I control them in a cage of love, I will be happy. This is a false statement. This Act, more than any of the others, caused me the most consternation and struggle. I was convinced that my happiness depended on others. I believed this wholly and sincerely from my earliest memory and all throughout my teenage years and adult life. I did things I would not have done, made mistakes I would not have made, and went down avenues I never would have, had I known that this statement is false.

If I can help you not to walk down the same roads as I have, then this book will have been worthwhile.

When we are brought up on the drug of approval and appreciation, one of the consequences of this upbringing is that we believe that when we act well and within the confines and constructs of how we are 'supposed to' behave, we will be rewarded, we will be approved and appreciated. To go against this concept will obviously lead to immediate castigation and ultimately cancellation. Irrespective of where we live in the world, or the type of society we live in, this statement holds true. It is truly ubiquitous.

.

As a result, we have a distorted view of love and happiness both within ourselves and in the world. I was convinced beyond conviction that my happiness would depend on others loving me. My life was dictated by the selfish, self-serving, and mostly ignorant belief that if I could do things good enough, or bad enough, to cling to people and make them love me, I would be happy.

I was wrong.

If you depend on others for your happiness you will never be happy. If you depend on others for your happiness, they will never be happy.

Why?

Because it is a cage.

Because it is an addiction. It is a drug.

Because you must constantly appease those people whom you wish to love in this way. You must gain their appreciation and approval. As you go through life this becomes increasingly impossible, and you become more and more dependent upon them. This is not love; this is possessiveness, this is control. Ultimately, it can lead to coercive control on your part, or the inverse in which you can be controlled very easily by someone who realizes that your happiness depends on them.

Love is the exact opposite of everything that you have been told. You have been told that it is 'all about me', the culture of me. In every facet of our existence, it is 'all about me' and 'what can you bring to me'. How can you love 'me' in this false commercial, consumeristic, capitalistic society which is full of lies? This is not the truth. Loving others is breaking down the cage.

'Show her you love her with diamonds' was a slogan invented by the diamond industry. 'Buy her a diamond', 'diamonds are forever', and 'diamonds are a girl's best friend' brought about the birth of the diamond engagement ring. This was only a little while ago, 1947 to be exact and it shows how easily we are fooled.

We all need to belong; we have an innate need to belong which goes back to our hunter/gatherer origins and much further back. When we do not understand that this is so, and we feel disenfranchised from society, then we cling; we believe all the conspiracy theories and all the social media constructs from capitalistic controllers, all of which bombard us to belong and be appreciated to be approved. This leads eventually to madness.

Why?

What is love?

Love is caring deeply for yourself and others so that you can set them free. You want them to shine, to be the best they can be, not for yourself or your own fulfillment, but for theirs. You want them to live their best lives, to do the best and be the best they can be or be the happiest they can be.

You are there to help them when they are in their hour of need. You don't need a reward for this. You don't need appreciation; you just do it because this is what love is.

We have confused love with infatuation or narcissistic possessiveness. If my happiness is dependent on others, then I must become a possessive, controlling, narcissistic clinging person. This will lead to madness, some sort of chemical or behavioral addiction, or narcissistic coercive control. Love is the absence of these things.

Love is freedom. Clinging, controlling, dependent love is slavery, and it will lead to your own destruction. You will build a cage, not of love, but of shame, of guilt, of pain and of need. If you want to be well, you must break down the bars of this cage. You must let the other person fly away. You must help them on their way and trust that they will come back (or not, as the case may be) because love is not about you. Love is about loving the other person or persons.

ACT TWELVE THE SIXTEEN
FALSE BELIEFS

IF I FOLLOW MY RELIGION, BELIEF OR IDEOLOGY WITH GREAT ZEAL, THEN I WILL BE HAPPY.

FALSE.

When our first cities and settlements developed, we started to develop a hierarchical structure, more discernible and more controlling than when we were nomadic hunter/gatherer tribes. The following statements will be covered in detail in the book *Wheel of Life*, but I will summarize as judiciously as I can in one paragraph the points pertinent to us here in these Acts. Why did we become more and more dependent on, and subservient to, human leaders and ritualized ideologies as our civilizations developed?

Let's examine how we arrived at this point in our history and see clearly why the 'need to protect territory' plays such a fundamentally important consideration when we try to understand ourselves, both in the dim past and today.

When Darwin developed his theory of evolution, following on from the discoveries of other naturalists, most of his observations of primates were carried out, not in the wild, but in a zoological environment. He concluded that the sexual urge was the main driver of all primates. Freud, and later others, developed this idea further. They concluded that most human problems basically stemmed from sexual conflict of one form or another.

Unfortunately for our understanding in the last one hundred years, this observation is completely wrong.

Anthropological studies and careful observations over the last seventy years, carried out in the wild, have conclusively shown that it is dominance (hierarchy) and territory that are the main drivers of all primates. All primates from whom we have evolved have a very strong hierarchical structure and a very strong sense of territory.

Because the numbers in a primate species group never exceeded more than a hundred individuals, hierarchies were developed with very little violence. This hierarchy was maintained by the group, not by the dominant individual, and although individuals changed in the group over time, it was the normative way that the group functioned. This hierarchial system can be traced back to fish, countless millions of years ago.

Similarly, territory is controlled by the primate group with great zeal. All primate groups will fight neighboring groups over territory. Usually, these fights or battles do not result in high mortalities, but instead reaffirm the territorial boundaries of each group.

These are the two main instincts in all primates: dominance and territory. We evolved from primates into *Homo sapiens*. They are equal in all of us as a species. I have told you this so that you recognize our deepest instincts.

In historically and scientifically observed hunter-gatherer clans, it has been seen that they usually number one hundred individuals and no more. Therefore dominance, hierarchy, and territorial disputes are relatively insignificant in mortality rates despite their deeply ingrained genetic imprint on us as humans.

You can now begin to see the problem, which is why I have told you this. As we developed into the first cities and city-states, dominance and hierarchy became more complex, more necessary and more controlling, since there were far greater numbers of people to deal with. So, we developed our first religions and ideologies, and they replaced our natural nomadic hierarchical structure with a contrived and controlling new structure.

The first city we know of was called Uruk, which developed about nine thousand years ago. Nine thousand years later, we have developed hugely in terms of technology, but as we can see if we look around the world, we have not really developed in any other way. In fact, we have developed extraordinary forms of state control and state intervention. We have developed extraordinary means of killing 'outsiders'. So, we have become the more advanced version of what we originally were: humans for whom territory is the paramount and preeminent consideration.

Our 'original sin', so to speak, then is our 'origin sin', i.e., we evolved as a species that will kill anybody and anything that gets in its way. Our modus operandi among ourselves is dominance, hierarchy, and territorial control.

Religion is a form of hierarchical control. You may not like this, but it is true. It has nothing to do with 'God'.

When we become aware and see the truth of this, we see how easily we were manipulated, and we see the dangers of all religions and ideologies. They are detrimental to us because they are acting on our 'origin sin', and our baser nature which we refuse to acknowledge. Now that we have begun to jettison religion we have embarked on an even more foolish belief, namely, our innate 'good nature'.

Now we live in a naive fantasy world where we believe that our own logic and instinct derives and determines our own morality. You can see the ludicrous nature of this position when we see ideologies and the horrors of the last thousands of years brought us, never mind this new ideology. You can also see that we need to evolve to see the truth of our situation and not a contrived one necessary during our period of evolution.

Then we will see the true nature of ourselves and our society. Then we will see why we act as we do: it is in our nature to behave in such a fashion. Our great hope is that through understanding truth and reality, we can overcome these elements of our identity and become attuned to the reality of what God really is. Of what truth really is. Of what reality really is.

Though this is just a very brief summary, it encapsulates us as humans. It shows us why we are the way we are and points a way forward with hope.

We have made quantum leaps before. We have come together in large disparate groups before, long before our first cities. We must learn to set aside our ideologies, religions, and differences, or we will be set aside as a species.

Why do we need and feel comforted by religion and ideology?

This is twofold. First, we all want to belong to something. A religion, an ideology, a belief, because we want to feel a sense of inclusion and the sense of power and empowerment that this brings; we believe that this will set us on the right path and the right thinking for life.

Second, it became apparent very quickly that it is much easier to control a big population in a sedentary setting when you have a hierarchical structure. We can see this from the Scorpion King in predynastic Egypt, through Sumeria, back to Ur and Uruk. The same patterns appear over a period of time of a stronger hierarchical setting based on kings, emperors, and priests. Eventually it results in the deification of the emperor, who becomes the highest of both the high priests and the secular leaders, and therefore he is rendered untouchable.

Our religion, our belief, and our ideology lay out in cogent, clear detail the rules we must follow, and we love rules, though we may say otherwise.

We love rules for how to behave, how to act, and how to think, because we do not want to think on our own. We want others to think for us, to tell us what to do because it is much easier. This is why our society at the moment is breaking down because we have unbelief or disbelief, and we have confused what belief is. We do not understand what belief is, and we don't understand the danger of ideologies and religions.

We have worshipped idols our entire history; we have never worshipped anything else. We never believed in anything except idols.

What is belief, and how does it make us happy?

Belief, as we understand it in our culture, is putting faith in a set of rules, set down by a religion, be it atheism, Christianity, Islam, Hinduism, or something else. It is also an ideology such as communism, Marxism, liberalism, socialism, wokism, postmodernism and capitalism. We can follow these rules clearly and we can have a sense of belonging, just as we belonged in our tribe fifty thousand years ago.

The problem is that this will not make you happy unless you are a very basic, stage one person without any nuance, or any questioning, or any need to live beyond a robotic existence. If so, then it will make you happy. For the rest of us, blind belief in a religion or an ideology is not belief. It is worshipping idols. This is how Nazism, communism, slavery, imperialism, war and genocide developed. We do obey and we are happy to follow blindly because we believe we are following the rules. If we have our 'god' on our side, so much the better; then we can do it with impunity and indeed approval in this world and the next.

You will, however, be just a brainless, addicted puppet, because all ideologies are about control.

It is important for our future evolution that we learn to develop as people. This programme gives you the power to develop nuance, to learn to discern, to try to understand what the truth really is, rather than what we have been brainwashed to understand the truth to be. In this modern world, people's lives are so meaningless, so controlled, and so unhappy. They cling to ideologies and religions because they have nothing left. They confuse this feeling of belonging with happiness. You need to understand that this is a very unhealthy situation.

True belief is knowing. True belief is acting when you have gone beyond cognitive thought and worked out intuitively how things really are. Accepting reality as it really is and believing it to be OK— this is belief.

It is obvious that unquestioning or convenient and habituated unthinking in the name of conformity and obedience is a false belief has been promulgated for the last ten or twelve thousand years, and we have been manipulated. We have also acquiesced and we bear responsibility ourselves. Our fears of other tribes, other nations, other colors, and other sexes are distorted, and our insecurities, our shame, and our guilt are manipulated by this worshipping of idols.

You must learn to discern and examine so that you can find the truth. To find the truth is difficult. There is only one way that you can learn the truth, and this is through either some sort of revelation or intuition; likely it will be by becoming aware through the suffering and pain you have experienced.

Our present dualistic-thinking process is false. There is more to life and to living than being right or being wrong. Our need to be right or wrong ('My religion is right, so therefore yours is wrong') gets us nowhere. These are man-made rules, and they are meaningless.

The only way that you learn the truth is through knowledge, leading to understanding, leading to awareness. Then you will see the truth, and you will see how we have worshipped idols for millennia.

ACT THIRTEEN THE SIXTEEN FALSE BELIEFS

IF I SACRIFICE EVERYTHING FOR OTHERS, INCLUDING MY CAREER, POSSESSIONS AND ASPIRATIONS, I WILL BE HAPPY.

FALSE

'I will go and give everything to the poor, I will sacrifice everything I have, I will do everything I can to help others, I will go and become a monk, a hermit. I will give my life for my country, my religion, my beliefs, and my ideology'.

You believe that this will make you happy, but it will not. This is a more refined form of possessiveness, but in fact this is itself a possession. It is a false belief; it is an addiction to approval and appreciation.

I have spoken to a great many people who followed this route but have not found happiness. Many very honest and very genuine people really believe this to be true. Are they to be judged and found wanting or simply wrong?

Well, we have learned not to judge anyone. We are in no fit position to judge since we are equally wrong ourselves. We are learning humility. Instead, we will ask ourselves what is really going on here and we will learn from it. Then we will be able to change. Eventually we will make our sacrifices worthy and not vainglorious. We will learn to distinguish the difference between acting to feed our outer false self and nurturing our inner true self.

Why is this a false belief?

The answer is that you do it for you; you do not really do it for anybody else. You do not give, you receive. It is the ultimate act of selfishness: you do it to make yourself feel good, to feel the drugs of approval and appreciation. You are getting your drug back in an even more refined form, with a higher level of intoxication and addiction. Everybody is telling you, 'How good you are', and 'How loyal, how true, how brave you are'. You feel great about yourself, you feel you are great, you feel you belong.

Murder in the Cathedral

TS Elliott wrote the play *Murder in the Cathedral*. The story and premise of the play is as follows.

Thomas Becket was a great friend and drinking partner of Henry II, King of England. He was loyal and true.

Because of the barons' revolt, and in order to keep the church on his side, Henry decided to make Thomas the Archbishop of Canterbury (head of the Christian church in England). By doing this King Henry thought he could control the wayward church and make the church do his bidding. However, when Thomas Becket became Archbishop, and even though he had not been a priest, he took the position very seriously and did not want interference from the king in the running of the church. This led to a steady deterioration in their friendship, ultimately leading Henry to remark 'this man is a huge obstacle who needed to be removed'.

Thomas Becket was aware of his position and the danger he was in, and his conscious conundrum was this: while remaining as Archbishop in the cathedral in Canterbury, knowing serious assault or death was imminent, was he selfishly seeking to become a martyr or was he acting correctly?

As with most great theatre, you make the decision yourself when you see the play.

Real sacrifice is in giving so that you can give to, or for, somebody else without any reward, purely for its own sake, because your life is not about you. It is giving without any drug of approval or appreciation, without any reward in this life or the next. Ultimately, if you do things for reward in any existence, you are acting selfishly.

'Oh, if I behave in such a way, when I die, I will be rewarded in heaven' is just another form of addiction. Heaven is all around you if you just lose your own false self, your own ego. You will never get to 'heaven' or be happy if you do things for selfish reasons. You need to reflect on this and see if there is any other reason why you are doing something. Is it for fame, for glory, to be appreciated? Because if this is so, you are doing it for the wrong reason. I am not saying that there is anything wrong with fame, achievement, and glory. However, if you seek these triumphs in any form, well that is fine. Just don't kid yourself about your reasons for wanting them.

This will not make you happy; it will just feed your addiction to approval and appreciation.

ACT FOURTEEN THE SIXTEEN FALSE BELIEFS

THE THREE CORE BELIEFS:

1. WHAT DOES NOT KILL YOU MAKES YOU WEAKER.
2. YOU ARE YOUR FEELINGS.
3. THE WORLD IS MADE UP OF EITHER GOOD OR BAD PEOPLE.

FALSE

By the time you have reached Act Fourteen of the false beliefs, you will begin to realize that life is more nuanced than you have been led to believe. It is not dualistic, it is not binary, yes or no, black or white, right or wrong. By now you will recognize falsehoods when you hear them or see them, and you will be able to view things with compassion, forgiveness, care and understanding. You will have begun to try to forgive and care for yourself.

What does not kill you makes you weaker.

Is this true or is it another false belief?

This is an increasingly insidious idea especially on social media and some modern thought influencers. It is yet another false belief.

This false belief is just another device to manipulate us. We know from science, and we know from physics that if we get an illness and we recover from it, we will be immune to it the next time. All suffering, if we learn to use it in the right way, will lead us to develop in a spiritual way, and grow out of this simplistic, drug-addicted, binary, dualistic way of thinking.

If I walk through my life constantly seeking happiness and pleasure, I will learn nothing. I will be a weak fool.

You might say:

'Look at the rabbit, the rabbit is innocent. How wonderful it would be to be a rabbit', and I will reply to you, 'Oh no, you are mistaken, because the rabbit is impotent, the rabbit can do nothing; and if you are a rabbit, you can do nothing'. Or you can be aware, un innocent. There are consequences to strength and loss of innocence. You can grow in awareness and become strong, you can deal with adversity, sadness, suffering, and pain. This will give you power because you will eventually realize that you can take responsibility, that you have power, and that you are capable of vast things. You can change what you do.

You will also see your dark side. You will realize that you could equally go out and do bad things, if you have not done so already; but while you are more than capable of doing so, now you choose not to do so. Therefore, you are neither weak nor innocent, you are strong. You have become strong through your pain and suffering. You have learned, and you are developing as a human being through stages to become a more integrated person. As you develop, you realize your capabilities (both good and bad) through experiential knowledge, understood if you like through cognitive intellect, but ultimately understood through gut, intuitive understanding.

You are your feelings.

'I feel awful.'
   'I feel overwhelmed.'
   'I feel minimized.'
   'Therefore, I am controlled by these feelings, and if this is how I feel, therefore this is how I must behave.' This is not true; this is just a surface grasp of life.

But you believe it. You believe it because you have been told that when you feel something, well then it must be true. It is not. This does not mean, of course, that feelings are bad, and this is why we become confused, as feelings are the way we feel.

We are not a slave to our feelings because we can change our feelings. We can change our feelings about anybody or anything or any situation. We can use our brains and our thinking to change our feelings, so that nothing or nobody has any power over us.

Take one example.

'I like Jim very much and I care very deeply about our friendship.'

Recently, however, I have come to realize that he has been having a secret affair with my partner, stolen money from me, and jeopardized my career.

'I don't feel good about Jim. I changed my feelings from caring to dislike'.

Why?

'Because I became aware of the factual information of the situation, and as a logical consequence I changed my feelings.' Do you see that! 'I changed my feelings.'

This shows that we can change our feelings. It also shows that feelings are not bad even if they feel bad, but because of our programming we are unable to differentiate between our feelings and thinking. I can equally say, 'My partner, my parents, my friend, my sibling have destroyed my life through a coercive controlling and abusive relationship, and I hate them. This feeling of hate is getting progressively stronger. The consequence is that this feeling is having an effect on me. It is making me feel ill, unstable, angry, and overwhelmed'. This feeling is getting me nowhere. I can see that despite the truth in it, it is a negative feeling for me. I must change it.

Thus, while feelings are very strong, impulsive, and irrational at times, sometimes they can be justified. However, for us to get well, strong feelings of hate must be changed, not so that we can feel good about ourselves, but so that we can free ourselves from the negativity associated with these feelings.

There is also another way of looking at it and though this is very difficult for us to understand, it is true. If I do not change these feelings of hate and anger and resentment towards Jim, then, most assuredly, I will take these negative feelings upon myself. Finally If I really love Jim as a friend, and irrespective of what he has done, and despite my angry, bitter, and resentful feelings, ultimately, I will still love Jim. When I now consider all this in awareness then I will make every effort to make sure that nothing happens to Jim, because now I have become free of hatred, bitterness and resentment.

But nobody has ever really told you this, have they? What is the message on all the movies, games, shows and news media we consume every day? They tell you and they sell you that you must always be angry, bitter and resentful, as it is normal. But it is not normal. You are behaving like a chimpanzee, our last common ancestor with primates fifteen million years ago, but you are no longer a chimpanzee; you are a human.

When you see that you are not your feelings, you can change your feelings with your thoughts. You can be free of all control, coercion, and abuse by doing this. You really can be happy in every way by learning how to effect the change that you are not your feelings.

The world is made up of either good or bad people.

Once again, this idea is very prevalent today, and indeed it has always been so. 'Them and Us.' Us in our clan and Them in their clan, and we pitch ourselves and our clan against every other clan. Our country pitched against every other country. Our religion pitched against every other religion. Our ideology pitched against every other ideology. We need to be right in this dualistic way of thinking. Everyone else is wrong. It is very simple and straightforward. It is very easy to follow this way of thinking, indeed anyone could.

There are obviously good and bad people, and we highlight this. Yes, we can see that there are people who behave *very* badly, but they are a tiny minority. However, as part of your programming, you will be controlled more and more as you go along. This has been done to us by the mythologizing of our past, the glorifying of our own race or clan, and the scapegoating of others so that we can be in control, we can belong. Yet we still need somebody to righteously vent our anger on.

So, we have the mythic slogan, 'We were once a great nation'. Nazi Germany, Britain today, China, Russia. You will hear such things from the demagogue who will ultimately be your controller and dictator.

What was taken away from you?

Who took it away from you?

Why was it taken away?

How was it taken away?

Who is doing it?

How can you get it back?

So now you are a victim, therefore you must identify with some-body else, as being in a group of victims. If you are a victim, then it is obvious that others are perpetrators. You are good, they are bad, and this means you are the good people, and they are the bad people; thus, you can feel good about yourself.

Having come this far in our programme, we now know that this mentality is one of the hallmarks of fascism, communism, or religios-ity. But you are becoming more aware, and you will not be subservient to or controlled by any of these demagogues or their ideologies. Instead, you will learn to stand your ground and speak clearly for the voiceless and dispossessed. Because you have been voiceless and dispossessed, you know the difference, and knowing the difference, you can make all the difference.

ACT FIFTEEN THE SIXTEEN FALSE BELIEFS

FEAR, WORRY, ANXIETY, LONELINESS, SORROW, VULNERABILITY, PAIN AND MANY MORE AFFLICTIONS ARE NOT A PART OF SUCCESSFUL LIVING AND SHOULD BE HIDDEN AND SUPPRESSED.

FALSE

'The world is full of sorrow. The cause of sorrow is attachment. The uprooting of sorrow is the dropping of attachments.'

— PADDY RAFTER

'The world is full of sorrow. The cause of sorrow is desire. The uprooting of sorrow is the dropping of desire'.

— BUDDHA

Fear, loneliness, sorrow, pain, and vulnerability are all part of the human condition. They are not afflictions. You have come to believe that they are afflictions because of your false programming. They are in fact positives, but you have been led to believe that they are negatives.

It is natural and right to feel fear. It goes back hundreds of millions of years in evolution, and as we evolved into primates, we developed our innate sense of fear in a very nuanced way. Fear is essential for our survival. When we see danger or sense danger, we either 'fight, flee or freeze'. This is normal, this is natural, this is essential. The problem is that this constant fear in today's society is killing us.

Worrying is the same thing. Worry is an ongoing fear. The pervasive intimation of some imminent danger you perceive is going to happen, or which may happen or could happen. It is always in the future. Sometimes our reasons for worrying are very clear and obvious to us, and sometimes they are not. Often, we just have an overwhelming sense of dread. We feel lonely, anxious, and vulnerable.

What we can take from this is that when we live our lives in fear and anxiety, we do not live in the present. Because we spend so much of our lives now in fear, worry and anxiety, we are never in the present, which means we can never live in peace and contentment.

We are bombarded with reasons to be fearful. Full-time news channels, social media, and legacy newspapers are always churning out bad news. Everywhere we look we see something to fear, or people to fear, people of a different color, race, religion, sexual orientation, etc.

This is an illegitimate fear born of manipulation by those in control, manipulating our programming and our desire to belong, so that we become confused. Therefore, we live in constant stress, and we think that by suppressing all these fears, anxieties, pain, loneliness, vulnerabilities, and other afflictions that we will be OK.

The truth is that the opposite applies. This is a part of the human condition; this is life. Accepting these sufferings and pain as they are and learning to accept them over a period of time changes us fundamentally and opens the door to our becoming more aware. They are the fast highway to a superior level of consciousness.

Suppressing fears and loneliness only exacerbates them, makes them worse, and makes them irrational, and has a particular effect on our mental, physical, and spiritual nature. It is the way of the world, and we must learn to show all our perceived negative emotions. Then we can drop them and grow; we can transform them and change their polarity into something positive instead of the negative we perceive them to be.

Understanding this is very important for us, as it is our way to start to become aware, our way to act, our way to change. We must learn to live in the present. Throughout our entire evolution, until twelve thousand years ago, fear was a transitory, fleeting thing.

The tiger attacked you or it did not. You died or you did not. You fought back or you did not. You froze or you did not. You took flight or you did not. It was over one way or another in short order, and you learned for the future to see the warning signs and not to go there, how to exercise caution, and this was your survival tool. Fear is meant to be a short-term mechanism for survival, and it is what allowed us to survive and evolve.

However, now we live in constant fear, always waiting for the tiger (metaphorically speaking) to come and get us. The tiger is not coming 99.9% of the time, so we live in apprehension for nothing. Our brain is so preoccupied with anxiety and fear that we have room for no other thoughts.

The reality is that everybody feels fear, anxiety, loneliness, pain and loneliness at various different times. In our world of filtered and edited online social media we see a fake narrative. Edited pictures and highlighted distorted stories give us a false impression. We then think everyone else is having a wonderful time and we are not. This is a false impression. This is a false belief.

We need to change. The way to change is to learn to live in the present, to accept where we are at this moment. I am aware of what may happen tomorrow, I am aware of what happened yesterday, but I am thoroughly aware that I am here in the present and that I can do absolutely nothing about yesterday or tomorrow. I may ameliorate the outcomes in one form or another. Since I am not in control of the world I cannot control its outcome, and so the whole process of fear and worry becomes obviously pointless.

Rooted in the now.

Living in the present means being rooted in the now, in the eternal now. There is absolutely no point in worrying about the future. This goes against everything you have heard. There is absolutely no point in ruminating about the past as you cannot change it. You must accept the consequences of your past with a 'super acceptance'.

Super acceptance

Super acceptance is a life skill that you must learn. It does not happen in a day. You must learn it over a period of time. Fear, loneliness, anger, hurt, vulnerability, sorrow, etc., if understood, can be and actually are very good for you.

This is because they tell you something about yourself that needs to be acted on if you would only listen to them and try to understand them.

Therefore, they are not afflictions, but they become afflictions when you suppress them.

ACT SIXTEEN THE SIXTEEN FALSE BELIEFS

YOUR LIFE IS A SHAMBLES, IN GREAT DISORDER, AND YOU ARE BLINDLY PARTICIPATING IN LIFE, ROBOTICALLY, TO ORDER, WITHOUT EVER THINKING OF WHY YOU DO WHAT YOU DO.

TRUE

So now you can see that we have come back full circle. Yes, your life is a shambles, but this time you admit it. You say, "Yes, I do feel shame, worry, etc., all these things. I did live in great disorder, and I did participate blindly, robotically, almost like a puppet, without ever thinking about my actions and their consequences. That is true, that is completely true.'

But the false part is that it did not and does not have to be this way. The very recognition of your life being a shambles, in great disorder, in whatever way you define it, is a great start. The fact that you have recognized that you have participated in a blind, nonsensical, disregarded life, causes you to say,

'Maybe I have been powerless to do something about it, but I know that it is different now. This is because I now have some knowledge and information that is helping me to have some form of understanding. With this understanding, I will then become aware.'

'I will cease to be a puppet. If I am not a puppet, then no addiction can have a hold over me. This will take a long time. I do not expect miracle cures, but I do expect that with time and increased awareness I will become well, and learn to live in reality, and to be able to see the world as it really is.

'I will be able to appreciate all the beauty that is in the world for what it really is. The world is existence; the human condition, being, and essence. I see that they are all interconnected, they all flows of energy.'

We can learn to experience life, not as a cacophony of noise, but as a song or a great painting. See and feel and experience the inherent beauty that is really there, in the world, in us and in nature. Learn to really appreciate everything, not by the adding of things, but by the subtraction of things.

PART IV

THE SIXTEEN KEY ACTIONS

ACT ONE THE SIXTEEN KEY ACTIONS

YOU HAVE COME TO THE REALISATION THAT ALL IS NOT
WELL IN YOUR LIFE. THIS MAY BE DUE TO ADDICTION,
DEPRESSION, ANXIETY, CONTROLLING OR TOXIC
RELATIONSHIPS, FEARS NAMED OR UNNAMED, TRAUMA
OR RESENTFUL DISSATISFACTION. YOU ARE SO UNHAPPY
AND YOUR LIFE IS OUT OF CONTROL.

Having come through the Sixteen Axioms and the Sixteen False
Beliefs, we have now come to the Sixteen Key Actions that
you can do to further improve your life and help you to achieve real
happiness and contentment. These are also the Key Actions that you
can undertake to regain control of your life and your interactions
with others. In time you can take positive, affirmative action that will
help you deal with your past mistakes, transgressions, and mess you
may be in.

I have deliberately interspersed throughout these Acts the
personal pronouns 'I' and 'we' to indicate that firstly, you are not
alone on this journey, and secondly, to show solidarity and the
connectedness of all things through the power of love. In a mean and

broken world, we can learn to seek beauty and love, thereby healing ourselves with this most powerful of all energies.

Actions do not always mean that we physically must do something. Sometimes they are just realizations or dawning's. You may become aware of something that you did not really understand until now. Sometimes the most powerful actions can be taking back control of your life, giving yourself a voice, and giving yourself your own responsibility. Thinking in a new way is acting in the most powerful sense. Learning to understand through intuition and gut knowing is the most effective realization of all.

Taking back responsibility and trying to find direction and meaning are our goals.

The difference now is we have a way of doing so. This will be cognitive awareness, because now we are beginning to change our perception of the way we see things and are more open to changing these perceptions. Hopefully in time we will have noncognitive, unfettered awareness and knowing, intuitive understanding.

Remember that the energy of love which pervades the universe is always available. I was cynical and nihilistic, wanting always to be right in a dualistic way, and always coming up with objections and dismissive rationalizations of the existence of any higher power greater than ourselves. I let my cynicism become my own ideology. If you have done the same, this new action will be difficult, but ultimately give you a rewarding new perspective. You are well aware of the negativity and the disdain with which we hold all authoritarian pronouncements or received purported wisdom. Arriving here, we lost much along the way. But having read through the previous Acts we now have a new perspective and a new understanding of reality.

'Wars, children with cancer, suffering and needless cruelty', we cried, as our proof of our ideology and disbelief. Yet we never realized that in our misconception and brokenness, we were the answer to healing these plights in our world.

The otherness, the one, the higher power, whichever term you prefer (I have told you before about the problem of naming things) protects you from nothing in this world, but ultimately sustains you in all things. We are powerful; we just refused to act on it, but now we have decided to act.

We cannot change until we realize that our perceptions may not align with reality.

We did not realize that we had become our own trauma.

We have come to the realization that all is not well. This can be in any shape or form, for any reason, and we have come to the realization that what we perceive to be reality has become our own trauma and pain. It can be anything: depression, despair, loss of family, loss of health, loss of self. We have fled to unreality because it has become too much for us.

We now have tools that can help. We have walked the walk, the trauma walk. This opened our hearts to have compassion for all people, and in time we will have compassion for ourselves. We found other ways to relieve the pain, whether through our maladaptive behaviours, drugs, alcohol, lifestyle, power, or money; all of these only led us to emptiness, to shame.

We have now accepted that we are unhappy. We do not have to judge what the unhappiness is, but we accept that we are unhappy (and maybe deeply unhappy), unmotivated, stuck in a rut, in deep depression, suicidal.

This is the first action: realization that all is not well. This is the most powerful act of all. It is an acceptance that all is not quite right. In time we will convert this tiny mustard seed into a massive tree of radical super acceptance.

ACT TWO THE SIXTEEN KEY ACTIONS

YOU ADMIT THAT YOU DO NOT UNDERSTAND THE REASON WHY YOUR LIFE IS LIKE THIS, OR IF YOU DO, THAT TO WHICH YOU ATTRIBUTE THE REASON WHY, IS PROBABLY INCORRECT.

From what you have been learning, you can begin to see that your perceptions and their objects are probably incorrect. We could go further and say, in most cases they are antithetical. However, we have built our lives around these incorrect perceptions. We built our lives around our wrong actions and inaction, and that has led us to a place where we now stand, where most of what we believed was incorrect, or we have understood things in a very wrong way, colored by the pain of our trauma and unwellness.

We must look deeper to find the truth. We must learn the value of silence, of silencing our mind, of quietness, of trying to meditate. Meditation is not a fancy New Age thing, but something that goes back to the dawn of current history and before. It just puts us in a state where we can remove our cognitive thinking process to some degree, so that we can understand intuitively whilst quieting our anxious mind, brain, body, and spirit.

This can be a difficult time.

When you initially come to this realization it can be very disconcerting. For some it can be a shattering experience because it can suddenly feel as if your whole life has been a lie, a failure. This is not true.

If you had not done the things that you have done, seen the things that you have seen, and behaved in the ways that you have behaved, you would never have been in a position to subsequently see where you are now.

You would never have been in a position to see your incorrectness and through life experience begin to change, to learn nonbinary thinking, to learn different levels of consciousness, to be an evolved human instead of a puppet. This is a really good learning opportunity, and a very positive thing.

When you come to understand that your reasoning and your attributions are incorrect at best or worse, deeply flawed, it is pointless to allow yourself to get bogged down. Over analysis is paralysis. We want to move forward; it is where it is, it is as it is.

This will take time. Through increased information and knowledge, you will develop awareness, and you will earn and learn radical total acceptance.

ACT THREE THE SIXTEEN KEY ACTIONS

YOU REALISE THAT YOU ARE LIVING AN INAUTHENTIC, FALSE LIFE, AND THAT YOU ARE UNAWARE AND LACK THE ABILITY TO LIVE IN THE WORLD.

This is a complicated act to dissect, because even though it sounds like a statement, it is an act. It is an act of realization through knowledge, giving you understanding. You realize you are living a false life, and that you are inauthentic to yourself. Therefore, you are something else, not you; you are living a false you.

If you are inauthentic to yourself, and are living a false life, it cannot be a life in which you are happy to participate. You are also very unaware, and you do not realize that this false life comes from your programming, of which (until now) you had little or no knowledge. This false life also comes from your addiction to the drugs of approval and appreciation.

We have come to understand our programming a little bit more throughout the previous Acts. We are starting to realize that a lot of what we believed about our lives, or thought we knew, was in fact untrue or irrelevant, robotic, and unthinking.

Taking this to its logical conclusion, the consequences of not becoming aware are that you either sleepwalk through a meaningless life and then die, or you examine life in a very superficial way. This leads you to live a superficial life with your false self, the outer self, the self-created by your programming and the drugs of approval and appreciation that you need so badly. You created a persona based upon your assumptions and addictions.

This may also lead you to decide that life is just about 'chaos' and 'random choice'. This is confirmed by listening to all the modern populist scientists on media, both social media and legacy media. This notion is everywhere, so you believe that all life is meaningless, and wonder what the point is of anything or anybody in the first place. This is nihilism, and it is endemic in our world. Nietzsche and Dostoevsky predicted something like this in the latter part of the nineteenth century.

If there is no meaning, then we create meaning out of ideology. Having spent the last millennia living in 'religiosity' and 'piety' instead of reality, conformity and being controlled was our lot. Religiosity and clericalism, which were totally controlled by men, was never about adhering to the real meaning of truth, but to rules and regulations, and worshipping idols. This does not mean that there were not genuine and honest people who adhered to religions in good faith. However, most of them were not so inclined.

We now worship another idol, the god of chaos, the god of meaninglessness, the god of 'it's all about me'. This ultimately leads to nihilism, deep depression and much more.

You live in a creation that you create.

Seeing the world as it is portrayed to you through your programming, and with your constant craving for the drugs of approval and appreciation, you have become unable to live in the world, as you only see it with your outer self, your false self. You are becoming increasingly dissatisfied with this way of living and with the person that you portray yourself to be. Therefore, when things become more and more irrational and meaningless, you must retreat to another world, the world of unreality.

How much you believe in an inauthentic and untrue life, or accept it, is directly proportional to how much you live in the real world and how much you live in the world of superficiality and unreality that you create in your own head. If you cannot see this, it is not your fault, because you have been programmed this way. Ultimately, if the life around you becomes meaningless, then the only way you can prove your existence is in superficiality, by building up the false self, the outer, shallow self of unreality, the 'I'.

We have begun to show here that the ideology of nihilism is a complete misconception, a mistake. It is of far graver concern because it carries within it an insidious and perfidious concept which is deeply damning to us as individuals and to society as a whole.

It is not science; it is not physics; it is an ideology perpetrated and propagated by those who are the new 'priests' and 'priestesses' of the world. These priests and priestesses are in science and physics fields, and their masters are in consumer, capitalist organisations.

If you believe that everything or anything is permitted, then anything can be everything, and all is a pointless existence except for ongoing satisfaction of the false self's cravings, which get worse day by day. Science is being used by certain controlling elements in modern society to suit their consumerist, commercial purposes. You are programmed to be a minion, a meaningless minion in the midst of this moral morass of pointlessness.

Don't be taken in by the modern, pervasive idea of 'our inherent human goodness', for as we have seen, we are the end iteration of an utterly ruthless species when it comes to clan and territory. We don't make nice rules. We do what we do to survive, to evolve. Were this 'naive human goodness' model true, then communist ideology would be a wondrous success. It is not. I have shown you why this is so.

Nihilism and meaninglessness are endemic in the constructed modern view of the world, so obviously the only ways you can react to it are either to create your own authentic world, or to live in a false world.

ACT FOUR THE SIXTEEN KEY ACTIONS

YOU RESOLVE TO EMPOWER YOURSELF THROUGH SELF KNOWLEDGE.

An unexamined life is a life not worth living. (Socrates)

A life lived falsely is by its nature meaningless. Given what you now know as evidence of your unhappiness, your dissatisfaction and malaise, you may now think,

'I am becoming aware that maybe there is more to life than that which I have been living. Maybe the information I have been receiving all my life is incorrect, maybe my perceptions have been incorrect, maybe my thinking is incorrect because of my programming. I am now realizing for the first time that I have been programmed. Maybe that is because of the world in which I live, with all its noise and nonsense that I hear repetitively every day, and which I absorb by a process like osmosis.'

Empower yourself through knowledge.

Therefore, you now resolve to empower yourself through knowledge, leading to self-knowledge and to self-examination. As I said, knowledge on its own can be used to manipulate us if we are on the receiving end, but if we are on the examining end we cannot be manipulated.

Again, I say to you: do not do this because I say it. Do not accept anything I say as the truth but examine it yourself. The truth will become apparent because the truth is the truth, and when you understand the meaning of the truth you will slowly gain self-knowledge.

How will you do this?

Through cognitive thinking, through intuition, through gut thinking, through learning how to think in a non-dualistic way. By learning to sit and meditate on the now; seeing, understanding and examining. You will begin to come to know who you are. You will also realize that you are not the person you thought you were.

You are not the alpha, false self you present to the world. Neither are you the drugged, articulate, or inarticulate fool who craves the drugs of approval and appreciation, and who is programmed like a puppet. Nor are you your attributions, your connections, your relationships. You are not the teacher, the chief executive officer, the professor, the bartender, the lawyer, the waitress, or the home carer. These are just the things you do. They are not you. You are not the sister, the brother, the aunt, the mother, the father, the wife, the husband, the partner, or the friend. All of these attributions are basically attachments; they do not define you. Though they are part of you, they are part of the outer you; they are not you.

Who are you?

If you have to describe who you are by your name, or by what you do, you do not know who you are. If you can describe yourself without such descriptors, you have begun to see what knowing and self-knowledge mean. Knowing means relinquishing, cleansing, and washing away all of the programming, ideologies and beliefs, and triteness that have been engendered in you since the day you were born.

Along this path of self-knowledge, you will begin through intuition and gut thinking to ask the questions,

Who are you?

Who am I?

What am I?

ACT FIVE THE SIXTEEN KEY ACTIONS

SEEK THIS KNOWLEDGE NO MATTER WHAT THE COST.

Seek this knowledge no matter what the cost! When you consider this Act honestly, this consideration will drive you, giving you motivation and strength. This is because it will be there in your consciousness, and in your subconscious, and in your makeup. You will want to do this, and you have to do this; it's the only way. You have been so unhappy for so long, there is no price that you will not pay to get well. This will motivate you bit by bit. Seek this knowledge everywhere.

Seek peace and stillness and quietness. Seek through meditation to block out your cognitive mind, your cognitive brain, so that your other understanding mechanisms can work, and you can know things differently, truly, as they really are.

I have made thousands of mistakes, and I have gone down very many wrong roads, not all in search of awareness and knowledge, and many times going nowhere. I did not know what I was doing. I was lost. In my very lostness, I discovered that this state of being was profoundly important, because then I could be found. I can only be found through my lostness, as can you. I can only see the light when there is darkness; the greater the darkness is, the more powerful and profound effect even a small light will have upon us. The worse we are, the easier it is to see the truth, because we have nowhere else to go, having seen through all the tedium and falsity of the false life lived by the false self, the addicted self, that leads us to perdition.

This programme that I am revealing or bringing to you will save you from taking very many wrong roads in wrong directions, taking many wrong turns, or taking the wrong fork. It will make it a little bit easier to follow a straight path. That does not mean the path will be easier; it just means that you will not have to follow a thousand other ones.

You will seek knowledge whatever the cost.

Who am I?

What am I?

You will do this with kindness. Yes, you will be very angry, and you will feel shame and guilt as you embark on this quest. This is the price we pay for seeing the true self. But you will also begin to see the real you, your true self, that has always been there since the day you were born.

Seek this knowledge no matter what the cost because there is no other way. There is no other way to be free.

ACT SIX THE SIXTEEN KEY ACTIONS

COME TO THE REALISATION THAT:

LIFE IS FULL OF SUFFERING

YOUR LIFE IS NOT ABOUT YOU

THERE IS A POWER GREATER THAN YOU

We have now come full circle, there and back again, the alpha and the omega. One of the primary things we have now realized is that, though we were in a sense addicted from birth, and though we have been programmed to varying degrees, all our information and knowledge was externally disseminated to us, and we took it verbatim. We understand that this is indeed the case for everybody, and we also see the consequences (both good and bad) of how we came to be where we were and are.

We are now able to see things more clearly for ourselves. For the very first time the veil is being lifted, and a new vista is being opened to us. This increasing clarity of understanding is crucial. Awareness is emerging in us, which is increasing our level of consciousness, building our inner, true selves, and discarding our outer, false selves. Therefore, we now know and accept that:

Life is full of suffering. We know this because we have been there. We have learned gratitude, Suffering has taught us much, We can now live having 'Peace of Mind, forged and annealed in the fires of pain and suffering.

Life is full of suffering still.

As we have read and understood all the preceding Acts, we have learned about the nature of things. The nature of humans and how we are in the world. It has also been revealed to us through cognition and intuition that the world is full of suffering. We have learned to accept this.

We understand enough by now to observe some crucial aspects of the human condition. We will never again waste our time engaging in pointless, fruitless arguments or semantics with ourselves or others about philosophical possibilities, religion, or science. We recognize these arguments for what they are. We recognize that fundamentally they are a glorification of the outer self and a vast ego trip. We will not be seduced by such silliness.

We will instead focus on reality. Only in reality can we be sure of where we are. All other avenues and roads lead us to perdition. We have understood and radically accepted the full, true statement we have made which is that life is full of suffering. We accept this because we know and have experienced for ourselves the suffering of life. Therefore, not only cognitively, but also intuitively and with strong gut feeling, we have brought ourselves to this point. Nobody else has told us what to do or how to think. We can now think for ourselves in many new ways and at many levels of consciousness.

We now have no problem accepting and indeed understanding the statement that life is full of suffering. We know this to be true, and we know reality. We know the way of the world now, and we will not shy away from our responsibilities in dealing with the world. We now readily recognize the vanities of the vainglorious. We also recognize and accept, radically, the value of suffering.

Your life is not about you.

Throughout our lives we have acted unconsciously, unknowingly, in unawareness. Truthfully, we have acted selfishly. We did not mean to, but there it is. Our pain and suffering, how we felt, the things that happened to us, and how our lives panned out—we can now see where all that brought us. Ambition and a wish to do well are laudable and necessary for us, and we do not decry them. However, we can now see, based upon what we have learned, that we have spent our lives feeding our outer selves, our false selves, and our ego.

We are by now aware of the consequences of such actions. They did not get us very far. At best we developed a very successful outer, false self devoid of any understanding and meaning. But we know in many, many cases our selfish actions have led us to terrible places. We also realize it was not our fault.

The outer, false self is superficial and selfish, and maybe we have taken that to an extreme extent. Nevertheless, we are now in reality. We recognize that selfishness is not the way for us. We reject the 'me' culture. Our lives were all about us, but we have now come to realize that we were the victims of our own selfishness. We can see that this paradox is fundamentally true. We also accept that this selfish self dies when we die.

Many of us died to ourselves a long time ago. We will now rejoice in living in a new way, in a forgiving and compassionate way, recognizing that when we give to others, we do it not for recognition or benefit but only so that we can grow. We want no approval or acceptance or acclamation.

We are now growing our inner selves, our inner consciousness, and raising our consciousness to much higher levels; this is a much greater recompense for us than any momentary gratification. We now know, or we are at least beginning to know, through intuition and gut thinking that this is the only way that we can be set free.

By having as our mantra 'our lives are not about us', the selfish part of us dies and the real part of us starts to live.

There is a power greater than you.

Rationalizations, placebos and wishful thinking now have no place in our lives. We see through them. Our suffering has taught us much. We have gone through the boundaries of ephemeral and existential thinking.

We are now rooted in reality. Our reality has revealed to us that there is, indubitably, a power greater than ourselves. We have seen it, we have felt it, and we have understood it intuitively, cognitively and with our deepest gut feeling. We are also not foolish enough to give it a name. It has no need for names.

We have also now come to understand that we can learn to connect with this power. We learn to align ourselves with it. In this alignement we become connected to the power of love which pervades the universe. We know that this is so because our experiences have taught us something of value.

Thus, we will dispense with suspense and disproportionality. We will dispense with pointless, ceaseless questioning. Even though those of us who do not know will act as if we do, until we truly do know. The action is key, not the thinking and there is nothing but boldness and bravery in making this attempt. We will do so many times. We will get better, As I have said, believing is acting. Finally, we have come to the understanding that we have a right to be here, a right to be ourselves, and that we are not random entities in a meaningless void.

Over time we will learn that we are part of the divine essence which permeates the universe. We will see that we are sacred, as indeed the world is sacred, and we will play our part to do what must be done.

ACT SEVEN THE SIXTEEN KEY ACTIONS

COME TO SEE THAT KNOWLEDGE, LEADING TO UNDERSTANDING, WILL LEAD YOU TO AWARENESS.

You will come to see that knowledge gained cognitively, experientially, intuitively, or by your gut will lead you to understanding, which will lead you to awareness. This understanding will need to be developed over a period of time. It will lead you to a greater understanding of yourself, the world, and your place in it.

This knowledge is multifaceted and comes in many forms, not just cognitive, experiential, intuitive and gut but sometimes it is transcendental. It cannot be defined but you will know with certainty it has grown in you. Awareness is all of these things and yet it is none of these things at the same time.

This understanding comes almost by unknowing. You must learn to clean the slate, to deprogram, before you can know.

This understanding of the many facets of knowledge is discussed in our earliest philosophical and religious texts. This is not a new idea.

We must learn the skill of unknowing, so that we can know. We must learn this by practicing silence, stilling our mind when we have knowledge, and working ever harder to get knowledge and understanding and become aware, so that it will almost become revealed to us through our work and through our stillness.

It is learning to plug into the energy of the universe which pervades every place we exist in all its forms.

ACT EIGHT THE SIXTEEN KEY ACTIONS

WITH COMPLETE HONESTY, EXAMINE ALL OUR
BEHAVIOURS AND MALADAPTIVE PRACTICES,
IDENTIFYING ALL SUCH BEHAVIOURS THAT ARE
LEADING TO SELF-HARM, DESTRUCTION AND
UNHAPPINESS.

Now that we are well embarked on our journey towards self-knowledge, external and internal, we now need to begin the process of self-examination.

How do we do this?

We must learn to be honest with ourselves and with others. We must honestly examine all of our behaviours and self-sabotaging practices and addictions. We will write them down and examine them again. We will identify every maladaptive practice, addiction, behaviour—everything that leads us to hurting ourselves and others, leading to destruction and unhappiness.

How have we harmed others?

By our actions and our unaware behaviour, we have wrought a trail of destruction. We have hurt everybody and hurt those closest to us the most. We have alienated people; we have damaged our interactions with our friends, our work colleagues. In fact, we have hurt everybody to varying degrees, not because we meant to but because we had to. Because we acted without awareness, in selfishness and thoughtlessness. Yes, we have done terrible things and we will atone and make restitution as best we can. Yes, we will redeem ourselves by our actions. Yes, we will make reparations wherever we can. We must also do the same for ourselves.

We are not at fault.

Though we are riddled with guilt, shame, and other attachments, and have hurt others and ourselves, we are not at fault here. This is the tragedy of our existence: everybody wants to blame us. They tell us that it is our fault and that we are addicted to a substance or a behaviour and this is our fault too.

We have heard it for years.

Now that we are on our programme, we see the effect that we have had on others and on ourselves. We feel shame and guilt, which makes us feel even worse. It is not our fault; we have now come to see that the fault lies with our faulty programming and thinking, and with the perceptions that subsequently programmed us in such a way that we had no awareness.

We hurt everybody because we were addicted. From our earliest memories and before, we could not cope with the world and our programming. We retreated to our castle in the air until this fantasy came crashing down all around us.

Now, however, having acquired information, knowledge, and the beginning of awareness, we are able to be responsible for all our behaviours and actions going forward.

So, with complete honesty examine all your behaviours. Write them down, examine them. Identify all maladaptive practices that led you to self-harm and caused destruction and unhappiness for both yourself and others.

ACT NINE THE SIXTEEN KEY ACTIONS

DECIDE TO CHANGE ALL SUCH HARMFUL BEHAVIOURS

Having understood, having reflected cognitively and intuitively, having acquired understanding and knowledge over a period of time, we have made our list, setting down in writing all harmful behaviours we feel we have. By now we have become more able to use knowledge to give us an understanding. We can see that these harmful behaviours are destroying us. The converse is equally true: we have learned that we are as important as anybody else, no more, no less, and we can see that we are worth preserving.

When we change these behaviours, we will know that we have put ourselves in a position to no longer be minimized, invalidated or voiceless. We are neither less than anybody else, nor more, but we are part of the universe. The divine spark is as much in you and me as in anyone else. We are part of the whole, and we have a right to belong and to get well.

We see that we are worth repairing, that we can make ourselves whole. We see that we can save ourselves from the unbelievable trauma and pain that we have gone through.

To do this we have to act; we must decide to change all our harmful behaviours. We will try from now on, as much as possible, to ensure that our behaviours will no longer harm other people or damage them in any way. We will also endeavor to stop damaging ourselves. All our harmful behaviours have been revealed to us from our own introspection in which we acted honestly, knowing that anything less would not suffice. So, we decide to act, we decide to change.

Once we make this decision, we become empowered. We will no longer be people blowing in the wind. Nor will we be at the mercies of other people, therefore other people will no longer control us.

We will see that neither those close to us, nor those in control of our governments, media, etc.. will decide our fate. By deciding to change our harmful behaviours, we will decide our own fate and take back our lives.

We will not change them all at the same time; we will change them one at a time. We will prioritize and start with the most important.

We will seek help however and wherever necessary.

We will be unafraid and unashamed to look for help, not only by plugging into the power of the universe, but also by looking for help all around us, because help will be there. For example, if we have substance abuse problems, we may decide we need an initial break and go to a rehab center or join a twelve-step programme. We will need support, so we will enlist people to help us, and their help will be there for us.

If we have maladaptive behaviours, we will equally seek support. We will seek the support of a therapist to help us and guide us if we need it, and we will enlist whatever other means necessary to help us to change. This programme is a very good means of help, but we need physical connection, we need each other. Many of us by now will have no family, no friends, nobody to talk to; we will be alone and feel despair and disillusionment, but help is out there. We must look for help wherever we can find it, it is our responsibility.

Once we decide to act, we decide to change, we can do so, and the answers will become readily apparent to us.

We will do it in small steps and small stages, building up our confidence one step at a time with reflection, understanding, and awareness within our hearts.

ACT TEN THE SIXTEEN KEY ACTIONS

RESOLVE TO LEAVE THE PAST BEHIND, AS IT NOW HAS NO POWER OVER YOU. CEASE TO IDENTIFY WITH IT, AND INSTEAD LIVE IN THE PRESENT, LOOKING FORWARD TO A HAPPY FUTURE.

This resolution, to learn to leave the past behind, is one of the most powerful of the Sixteen Key Actions that we can do for our recovery. I found this Act particularly difficult for myself, as I regurgitated, ruminated and regretted all the past errors I had made and all the hurts I had perpetrated on others through my ignorance. These mounted up over the years, and my shame and guilt became ever more powerful and strong, so I lived in the past.

I lived in what I call the Five Rs:

Rumination

Regurgitation

Regret

Resignation

Resentment

This way of living destroys our lives. One of our great tragedies is that we are unaware that we are constantly living in the past. We do not talk about it, but we constantly regurgitate it. Now, having read these Acts and gained knowledge, we understand the real power of the past and its negative connotations. This does not mean that we will not learn from it, and this does not mean that we will not be aware of it. But we will never again be afraid to take it out and look at it, because we will have examined it honestly and taken ownership of it.

This means that when the past recurs (which it will) and we are confronted with our previous misdemeanors, bad deeds, mistakes, shame, or worse, we will not be afraid of the past anymore.

It will cease to have power over us because we have taken responsibility for it. Nobody can hurt us because we know it and we have let it go, which is the key Act. It is now in the place it should be: in the past. The past is not our eternal present. We can do nothing about it, except take responsibility for it, and ameliorate as best we can the consequences of our actions.

We will seek out those we have hurt. We will seek out those whom, through our ignorance and our addiction, we have damaged, and we will try to make amends with them as best we can. Unless seeking them out to make amends will make matters even worse; then we will leave it.

We will do this honestly, and we will do it with the beginning of wisdom, knowing that we also will not engage with people from the past that we should not engage with anymore. Now that we have the beginning of wisdom, we will know when to approach people and when not to do so.

We will be unafraid of the responses of those whom we have hurt or damaged, knowing that for us to get well we must accept where people are coming from, and not everyone will thank us. The good part of this key action is that we will find kindness and understanding as well.

We do this not for ourselves and our ego, but to make amends, and to help us to live a proper life. A life worth living, a life that befits a human being, not the life that we have lived heretofore. A life where the past holds no fear.

The greatest creator of our fears is the past, our past. We need to own our past. We fear what is in our future based on what is in the past. Therefore, it becomes obvious to us that we have either been living in the past, or in the future, and in fear either way. The fear of what we have done in the past, the fear of what may happen in the future. This is a living hell, this is a nightmare, and you are not where you should be.

Drop clinging to the past as in a bizarre way we become addicted to it and we are, once again, in chains. Work on it. Let it go and be free!

Where you should be, and where you will be well, is in the present.

When we have begun to understand and carry out these actions, we know that we can look forward to a future that can be happy for us. This is because we suddenly realize that we can be happy in all circumstances. We have learned to drop all attachments. Attachments to our fears, our resentments, our resignation. Thus, we can see the negative power in all our lives of the Five Rs.

Rumination

Regret

Regurgitation

Resignation

Resentment

We can transmute these into a new 'R'. We can 'Resurrect' ourselves, and we can be whole. We can 'Recover' and be made whole.

We will not fear the past, nor will we fear the future. Nothing will ever have the power to harm us again. This is the greatest of all gifts that we can have. The past has its place, and the future we can plan for, but we will learn, and we will act to remain in the present.

The present is our key action.

ACT ELEVEN THE SIXTEEN KEY ACTIONS

TAKE RESPONSIBILITY FOR ALL YOUR ACTIONS, PAST AND PRESENT, IRRESPECTIVE OF WHAT THEY ARE, AND CEASE TO BLAME OTHERS. DECIDE TO GET RID OF ALL RESENTMENTS, JUSTIFIED OR UNJUSTIFIED, SEEING THEM FOR THE POISON OF THE SOUL THAT THEY REALLY ARE.

This is an essential part of our Key Actions that we must be specific about. The reason we must be specific about this is because resentment is poisoning our soul, our mind, our thinking, and our health. It is making us spiritually, emotionally, physically, and mentally unwell. We must name it specifically as an action. Responsibility is one of our best ways to deal effectively with the resentment in our lives.

Failure to take responsibility for our actions is catastrophic for us. Deciding to get rid of all the resentments that we may have is essential, because we will see that we have many resentments against other people, places, and situations. But ultimately, we will see that the biggest resentment we have is toward ourselves.

Take responsibility for all our actions, past and present.

We take responsibility for all our actions, past and present.

This is the first part.

What we did in the past we did in ignorance, in unawareness, and we are truly sorry for it. We will make amends, both for anything we have done in the past that is wrong and to the people we have hurt. It is important to remember that we have also done many good things in the past. They should not be forgotten. We are not all bad. We will realize that we are human, acting ignorant, acting unaware because of programming and our addiction to approval and appreciation. We may also have suffered from substance addictions, behavioral addictions, and addictions of the mind and the soul.

Only we know the real truth. That means we have the real power, and this power makes us the true arbiters of our future, by taking responsibility, by being ourselves.

We are now constantly examining, and this is becoming a part of our daily life. We examine on a daily basis, we reflect, and we think with our gut, head, and heart. We know exactly what other people have done and what we have done.

We take responsibility for our actions, good and bad, past, and present, irrespective of what they are. We cease to blame others irrespective of what they may have done to us or not, because the only person that suffers when we blame others is ourselves.

We will not be foolish; if others are indeed to blame, we will attribute to them what they may have done wrong or that which we perceive to be wrong, but then we will drop it and drop our resentment of it. We then disidentify from these people, and we cease to blame them.

We will always be in reality, We will try always to act with kindness and compassion.

Whatever reality we understand, or whatever perception of reality we understand, we blame nobody, including ourselves, anymore. We learn to let go; we learn to forgive. By taking responsibility, in honesty and compassion, we find ourselves empowered.

We always remember that taking responsibility is not the same as blaming or judging. We take responsibility in the absence of blame, in the absence of shame, and with the desire to be well and to live a life worth living.

As we forgive others, we forgive ourselves. The more we forgive others, the more we forgive ourselves. The more we can free ourselves from the chains of hate, the more we can become well, as self-hate is the hate that binds us most.

Forgiveness is the most difficult action you will ever do.

All our resentments are deeply damaging to us, so we must get rid of all of them. This is true even if we feel they are fully justified. Fundamentally they are all damaging, and we must discard them. We can now see them for what they are, for what they truly are, because we are becoming more open and aware.

We can see that resentments and blame have been used in every justification, every war, every hatred known to humans. These are where evil resides in the world. We blame others, we blame minority groups, we blame somebody of a different skin color or a different sexual orientation, someone wealthier, someone poorer, for our problems.

We blame what people have done to us in a personal sense, whether by our partner, our parents, our brothers and sisters, our aunts, and uncles. We blame everybody and anybody because we do not want to take responsibility for ourselves. Because it's easier that way. Because it's lazier and unthinking. But deep down we really blame ourselves. We are not going to do this anymore, so if we forgive others and forgive them well, we can forgive ourselves and be set free.

ACT TWELVE THE SIXTEEN KEY ACTIONS

RESOLVING TO BECOME YOUR TRUE, INTEGRATED, AUTHENTIC SELF, YOU WILL ENDEAVOUR AS MUCH AND AS THOUGHTFULLY AS POSSIBLE TO MAKE GOOD THE HARM YOU HAVE CAUSED TO OTHERS.

This is a most specific Act, specific and necessary for our wellness, so that we can unlearn unhappiness and just accept happiness. We must remove all the layers that we have built on top of our faulty programming over many years.

When we become our true, integrated, authentic selves, we will have more self-growth within us. We will learn to be more honest with ourselves and with others. We will take the time to examine our own actions, faults and behaviours. We will endeavor to make good where we have been wrong and where we have hurt others. This is how our true, integrated, authentic selves blossom.

This is one of the few things that we have power over; remember, we learned earlier that we do not have power over anybody else, just ourselves.

We will try to repair relationships and hurts, recognizing that it is we who have been wrong. Though we may meet rejection, we will be undaunted. Since we do not seek approval, we will right what wrongs we can in an honest way, knowing that this is all we can do and that it will suffice. Remember that there is also good in the world; help and compassion will come to you from the most unexpected places.

We will try, in a thoughtful and honest way and as much as we can, to help others, because it is in helping others that we help ourselves.

We do not help others to make 'us' feel better; it is not about us, it is not about the external self.

We do it because it is the right thing to do. You do it to promote the growth of the inner self, the authentic self. No longer will you look at things in a binary way, (black and white)but you will have compassion for yourself and for others and for all situations, realizing that you are an integral part of the whole and you have a right to be here. It is not about you, but it becomes about you. The real you. This is the key, unknowing.

We do not know what may happen or how things work out but we do the right thing anyway, as best as we can, and we do not worry about the outcome. Just as we now embrace deferred gratification when before we could not wait a minute for satiation, now we embrace unknowing.

When we do this we become close to reality through the centrality of reality, energy, and existence. We are in the world in reality, honesty and truth, because we have discovered what truth really is. We have discovered the power of love that permeates the universe. We will be able to stand back and see a tree, or a flower, or any situation, and we will see all that is in that one thing.

ACT THIRTEEN THE SIXTEEN
KEY ACTIONS

LEARN UNCONDITIONAL ACCEPTANCE OF HOW YOU WERE, OF WHAT HAPPENED TO YOU, AND OF HOW YOU HURT OTHERS. FORGIVE YOURSELF AND OTHERS; FORGIVE THEM ALL.

I am so aware of how difficult this Act is. This is an Act of continued action, over many years. We will come to recognize the enormous importance to us of the contents and the fulfillment of this Act. We have dealt with a lot of aspects around this wholly crucial Act and now we must begin to enact it,

I know that this Act is the hardest thing for us to do for very many reasons. Having come this far, we know what these reasons are. I have been intimately acquainted with a lack of self-acceptance, and self-hatred and fear. In the depths of despair, hate and self-loathing, I discovered something. This discovery changed my life, and it will change yours. We need to be blunt and honest here. Nothing less will suffice.

Self-loathing, self-hate and the resentments they implied became the fuel for my destruction. Self-, loathing and self-hate are just other forms of resentment. The only difference to any others is they are resentments of self. Like any other resentments, we must release them.

What exactly do I mean by the implications that self-loathing, self-hate, and resentments bring? Through these Acts we have understood our initial state and our initial addiction to the drugs of approval and appreciation. Our programming compounded this. In our case, for reasons that are unimportant now, we went on a spiral of destructive thinking, maladaptive behaviours, and addiction of one form or another. This is a perpetual cycle. One day I saw the truth: I was my own destruction. I was, and I fed, my own addiction.

Equally, loathing and hatred of others and the resentments they implied became the fuel for my destruction.

What exactly do I mean by the implications that loathing and hatred of others and resentments bring? Though my loathing and hatred of others may have been initially justified, the spiral of negativity they created eventually became my only reason for everything. Those feelings became the reasons for my addictions and maladaptive behaviours. Their initial righteousness, real or perceived, became a masquerade. They were the product of bad thinking and false beliefs, fed by addiction superimposed on earlier addiction, trauma, and programming. One day I saw them for what they really are.

They were the means of my self-annihilation.

Having come so far in the 48 Acts, we now recognize certain key features. We now recognize truth and reality and are unafraid to name them. Therefore, we see the following, and this applies to us all:

We had no self-acceptance, and we had no ability to acknowledge how we had hurt others. This is because we lived in fear all the time. Totally absorbed by and living in our false selves, we were unaware of our true selves, or even in many cases did not realize that our true, inner selves existed at all. We had hurt other people so much. That is a fact that is unavoidable. Though we know we should and must try to make recompense for all our transgressions as best we can, nevertheless we must recognize that we are powerless over the things that happened. The things done by us. The things done to us.

We radically accept that we were hurt and traumatized and that we also hurt ourselves; this is a fact, it is unavoidable. We also radically accept that we hurt others and caused a trail of destruction in many cases. This is a fact, it is unavoidable.

In order to live free and happy lives, we must free ourselves from all of this baggage, which is really resentment and attachment.

How can we forgive ourselves? How can we accept ourselves?

We must recognize that we overuse our hurt by others as an excuse. We had become addicted to hurt. Now we can see hurt for what it really is. We see it for the poison that it really is. We can see it is an excuse, a drug, just like any other addiction. It is our dishonesty masquerading as continued pain, unrelieved and undiluted, but it is nevertheless an excuse, and we must drop it.

We can only be free from trauma when we cease to let it have power over us. We need to learn unconditional acceptance—radical acceptance, super-radical acceptance—of how we are. Only through acceptance can we be authentic.

We have become aware that we fundamentally are, and have been for a very long time, creatures made up of energy and faulty programming. We are habituated through our drug and our programming. We need to radically accept that and get into reality.

When we were very unwell, we were unable to have any form of acceptance on our journey, because we lived in pain and ignorance. But now, on this journey, we will learn unconditional acceptance of how we were and how we are, of what we did and what happened to us, of when we hurt others or when we were hurt by others. We forgive them, and we forgive ourselves. I am only too aware of how difficult this is and how long it may take you, but you must do it. You must do it for you, to be free.

We will have to do this every day for the rest of our lives. This is as necessary for us as breathing. If we do not, this tight chain will choke us, and we can never be set free.

The only way to unbind ourselves is by constantly working towards unconditional, radical self-acceptance, through stillness, meditation, quietness, and solitude. Understanding through our intuition and our gut, and not by rationalisations. Reflecting honestly and daily on how we can improve for others, how we can improve for ourselves.

As we work, we will become free and know that which we never knew; we will know peace of mind, we will encounter it and have serenity. We will live in reality and in harmony with ourselves and others.

ACT FOURTEEN THE SIXTEEN KEY ACTIONS

YOU WILL CONTINUE EVERY DAY TO WORK ON YOURSELF AND SELF-REFLECT. TO REALISE THE DIVINE SPARK OF GREATNESS WITHIN YOU. TO LOVE YOURSELF AS YOU TRULY ARE, ACCEPTING THAT THERE IS INALIENABLE LOVE AND TRUTH IN THE WORLD.

You have led yourself to this point. You have arrived here yourself. I have not led you; nobody has indoctrinated you to come here. You have self-realization. By following this programme, you are becoming aware. You do not need a medium. You do not need an intermediary to tell you what to do. You know what to do yourself. You are the sum of all parts, and you are becoming aware.

You have come to this conclusion yourself, not because I have said it. Indeed, it is you that has uncovered yourself, and come to the awareness that your life is worth living. You have rejected invalidation. You have seen that we are all valid.

Every day you must work on self-reflection. You now know that the divine spark, the energy of the universe, is within you, and that you have every right to exist.

Greatness is within you, so you can now do whatever you feel is the right thing to do while trusting in your decisions. Not because of the 'I' and your desire that your life should be about you, but because this is the right thing to do, and you know it. You may make lots of mistakes, but your intentions will always be towards others, towards greater good, and you are empowered by the energy of love in the universe.

You will learn to love yourself as you truly are, knowing that you are a part of the love that is in the world. You will know that in essence we are love, and since we brought evil into the world, we can also bring love. These are energies, and we refute evil with our power of love.

We have the power to choose. We are no longer a leaf blowing in the wind. We are no longer helpless. We are empowered.

You will accept this because you know. You have begun to think in a nonbinary way, and also to understand that you can intuit many things that supposedly cannot be understood, by gut understanding. You have begun to become aware by practicing 'unknowing' as we have defined it. You are at this point not because you have been indoctrinated, but because some understanding has been revealed to you and you have become aware. You will know, in some almost unfathomable way, the inalienable love and truth in the world.

This realization changes our lives because we have come to it on the path of truth. Nobody else told us or beat it into us. We reject ideologies, we reject idols. Nobody has radicalized us. Nobody is controlling us. We have arrived here by our path of pain toward wellness.

We will see with a 'Big Seeing'. We will use our higher consciousness for the betterment of others. We can bring about change in the world around us. This is because by now we can see that a lot of people in the world are very unwell.

Now we ask what we can do about it. People are unwell in so many ways, and our society is so unwell.

We now recognize the cynicism and skepticism in the constantly repeated refrain, 'Oh well, this is all meaningless, useless, there is nothing I can do, I am powerless!' We recognize this as a reflection of what is causing our society to be so sick in the first place. Empowered and growing as we are now; we will not abnegate our newfound responsibilities. We will repudiate the pervasive negativity promulgated in our world by responding, 'No, there is a lot we can do!'

We know powerlessness and we know power. We can do a lot; we can change the world because we have divine energy within us. The energy of the universe, which we have realized for ourselves. We have become the energy of love.

We can see that our planet, its climate and ecosystems, and all facets of our way of life are so fragile. The world is a macrocosm. It is like one big biological person. It is a manifestation of energy, just at a greater, bigger level.

So now, by growing in awareness and imbued with understanding we can act appropriately. We can act to change the world for the betterment of others. We can trust ourselves because we have suffered.

We can use this suffering to change the world.

We can also finally answer the question we have often posed in these Acts.

Who am I?

'I am the underlying consciousness in which perception happens.'

Or we might rephrase it another way: 'I am a consciousness that is inextricably part of the consciousness of the universe. The consciousness of all things.'

ACT FIFTEEN THE SIXTEEN KEY ACTIONS

HAVING GAINED MUCH GREATER UNDERSTANDING AND REALISING THAT THERE IS A FORCE FAR GREATER THAN OURSELVES, WE WILL PERCEIVE THAT THIS POWER WILL HELP US WHEN ALL ELSE FAILS, IF WE JUST ASK. HAVING KNOWN SO MUCH PAIN AND TRAUMA, WE WILL KNOW THAT HUMILITY IN ITSELF IS NOT HUMILIATION. THUS WE WILL LOOSE THE CHAINS THAT BIND US, AND WE WILL BE SET FREE.

We have come full circle, and we are now renewed and new. We have left behind our outer, false selves, fed with lies, programmed, and filled with wishful, fanciful thinking. Our outer false self has lost its power and our addictions have no power over us anymore. Our maladaptive behaviours no longer control us because these maladaptive behaviours work on our outer false self and as we have seen, this false self is ever more weakened as we work on our Acts every day, This outer false self is the self that dies when we die, so we will not feed it anymore. We will nurture our inner self so that we may live.

Now, we have gained great insight, through knowledge, reflection, intuition and understanding, and we now realize that there is a force in the world, an energy far greater than us. This will help us when all else fails.

This energy, this otherness, this higher power (choose whatever name you like, as we have realized that names are meaningless) protects us from nothing, but ultimately sustains us in all things.

We have walked the walk, the trauma walk. Our hearts are open to compassion and understanding for other people. This force of love, of energy, surrounds us; we can plug into this energy at any time, and it will help us.

This is very logical. The programming and the addiction to the drugs of approval and appreciation have no power over us anymore. The essential truth is what matters.

Without anyone telling you, you have become aware. You have become aware of all the lies, the deceit. You have seen the truth and intuitively know what the truth is.Therefore you know that there is a power greater than anything. This is the truth.

I have one more practice to share with you, one more 'R' to share with you and it's the one I consider most vital:

Repetition.

I use repetition. I remember one concept that I must have heard a thousand times and on the one thousand sand first time I listened and understood it.

We must repeat our practice of these Acts every day to get well and to stay well. Remember, it took us a long time to get unwell. It will take time, constant repetition of the actions and reflections in these Acts, and practicing them daily to get well and stay well. This is the essence of what 'mindfulness' is in a real way, away from all the marketing and the rubbish.

Knowing all these things begets humility, so we have become humble. We know that we are neither greater nor lesser than anybody else. We also know that humility is not humiliation; humility is acceptance, knowing who you are, knowing where you are, and knowing your situation in the world and being happy and content in it.

Since we now have peace of mind, and we have paved the way to happiness and enlightenment, we need never again be unhappy in our entire lives. We need never fear again.

We who have known so much trauma, hurt, pain, hate and all of the other negatives, have learned that we can now know peace. We recognize truth and honesty, and we experience freedom.

We can live with ourselves and others in reality.

ACT SIXTEEN THE SIXTEEN KEY ACTIONS

GET INTO REALITY, BECOME AWARE.

Having reached this point, we are becoming more aware. We are not asleep, and we are not living robotically or in a programmed manner. We are living life, living life to the full. Living life with joy, peace and happiness.

We are busy with life. We are immersed in life. We are in harmony with the great song of the universe, and with the great singer of the song.

We are the song, we are the singer, we are that which is sung, and we are none of these things.

We have become aware.

PART V
CONCLUSION

Now that you have read through and begun to understand the 48 Acts and all that they contain, the first thing that I would like to do is thank you for reading them. You have made a good start. The next thing that is imperative is that you begin again.

This time, stop more often and take more time to reflect and consider. To envision how the Acts may pertain to your particular circumstances. Over a period of time and with increased familiarity you will be able to partake in these Acts in a deeper way. You will see with a Bigger Seeing. You will know with a different type of knowing.

This will become apparent to you over time. Reflect on and partake of and participate in these Acts every day, as I do. Only in this way can we get an authentic path to our true, inner selves, in reality.

When you feel ready, it would be helpful for you to read *The Wheel of Life*. This book expands on certain areas of these 48 Acts and delves in greater detail into the more metaphysical side of our nature.

I hope these 48 Acts will encourage people to form a support community. This supporting community will have as its primary function a repository of knowledge and wisdom for all of us. This support community will be a renewed source of community for all.

This community and support structure is something which is so badly needed in a world where community is dying, and isolation is the new normal. We know just how detrimental for us as individuals and our neighborhood and society at large this is. It will also be a place of rest for all of us. I hope that we can form communities that reflect the values contained in the 48 Acts. I hope then, over time, we can bring these communities to every country, city, town, village, and house in the world.

I hope that by partaking in and reading these Acts your life will be changed immeasurably. Remember this: remember the interconnectedness of all things. Remember the power of love that pervades the universe and every fiber of our being, Remember there are many ways to know. Remember finally that you are of inestimable value and that by dying to your outer, false self, you have been born to your inner, true self. Therefore, you are part of the interconnectedness of all things.

APPENDIX

The scientific or medical perspective

It is very important for us to understand what exactly is happening in our bodies when we are in active addiction from a chemical or behavioral stimulant. We need to have a basic understanding of what is happening in our body and in our brain, and of our total body responses to stimuli and why they occur.

While this is imperative knowledge for those who are in active addiction or who feel they may be on a cusp toward a more dangerous addictive level, I am certain that it is equally important for everybody else because, as you will see, we are all addicted to something.

Those of us suffering from depression and anxiety will also gain a tremendous basic understanding of the chemical processes in our bodies.

On our path towards wellness and freedom from these afflictions, we also become aware of a vitally important fact. We see what medicine can do for us and how it helps us. More importantly, we see why medical intervention in addiction has such a tiny success rate.

With depression, for example, we see and understand the limitations of tablets and chemicals. The pharmacology industry makes billions and billions of euros or dollars every year from these types of afflictions: depression, anxiety, and addiction. While it is necessary in some cases to immediately have direct, short-term medical intervention (and this is to be encouraged), in the long term these types of treatments will not work. Understanding what's happening from a scientific standpoint shows the limitations of these chemicals. Fundamentally, we are treating the symptom and not the cause.

Therefore, you will see how the 48 Acts are so vital for us today to be well and to stay well in the long term. Our goal is a long-term solution towards wellness and happiness, free from depression, anxiety, addictions or any other behavioral maladaptations.

Understanding this will also demonstrate something else. We have the power within us to heal ourselves.

The simple science

Dopamine is the learning neurotransmitter. It is the positive-reinforcement transmitter. It is the transmitter that tells you, 'This feels good, give me more.'

Serotonin is the opposite. It is the neurotransmitter that says, 'This is good. I don't want or need any more.'

The problem is that from childhood we have failed to distinguish between these two. They are clearly different things, and our inability to distinguish between them is not our fault but is due to our faulty programming. The consequence of this is that we continue to try to reward ourselves forever for the wrong reasons.

There is a third hormone or neurotransmitter that is not often mentioned, and that is cortisol. Cortisol is the stress hormone. It works on your prefrontal cortex just behind your forehead. This is the rational part of the brain that helps you make rational, correct decisions.

When we become severely addicted, depressed, or anxious over a prolonged period of time due to stress and trauma, then our prefrontal cortex becomes damaged.

As a result, we are unable to plan ahead, to see the future. We can only function from moment to moment. The consequences of this are simple to understand. Irrespective of what may happen in the future, we cannot see the future, understand it or grasp it. Instead, we want our reward now.

We are then completely unable to defer gratification. That causes our dopamine to work even more strongly and with an immediate effect on us. This extreme overactivity over a prolonged period of time leads to actual cell death. Therefore, it is this endlessly repeating cycle or combination of dopamine and cortisol that leads to or deepens our addiction.

It is that simple.

As individuals and as a society we are becoming more and more chronically stressed and traumatized. We need rewards to cope with the stress or trauma of daily living. Thus, we are drugging ourselves.

As this becomes more pronounced and the damage more evident, we retreat to our primitive brain which is not very good at making forward-thinking decisions.

Equally, an imbalance of serotonin and cortisol also causes effects in us, the main one of which is depression. Serotonin binds to its receptor and inhibits neurons. Cortisol reduces the function of the receptor, which means less serotonin is actively available to our brain. Therefore, we get less serotonin effect, and this causes depression.

The most important thing we must understand here is that due to our programming and the trauma we have experienced or are experiencing, plus the environment of extreme stress we live under in the modern world, we are producing more and more cortisol. This is reacting with dopamine and serotonin, causing our addictions and depressions in a chemical sense.

The reward system is vitally important for us as it gives us the impetus to do everything positive in our lives, from getting up in the morning to working, taking care of ourselves, and functioning successfully in every other facet of our lives. Reward is essential.

The problem arises when we overcompensate and give ourselves pleasure as a reward. Due to our programming, we are in many cases unable to distinguish between reward as pleasure and reward as happiness.

Therefore, we become confused and lost, unable to distinguish between the two concepts: pleasure as reward and happiness as reward. This leads to addiction, maladaptive behaviours, anxiety and depression.

Pleasure is short-term, whereas happiness is long-term.

Pleasure is sensory, whereas happiness is not sensory.

Pleasure is all about me and what I can take for myself, feeding my outer, false self. Happiness is in what I can do for others and making my life not always about me.

Pleasure is something I do on my own, whereas happiness is me being part of something bigger than myself, with others.

Pleasure is achieved or attained with substances or maladaptive behaviours, whereas happiness is natural.

Fundamentally, we can narrow this down from a scientific point of view that pleasure is dopamine and happiness is serotonin. The catastrophic catalyst is cortisol.

Dopamine excites neurotransmitters, and the more you get the more you want. This is because the brain has a safety measure that cuts down the effects of dopamine on the neurotransmitters, causing you to need more for less and less effect. Otherwise, the brain becomes overstimulated, and the cells die.

We who understand chemical addiction recognize this all too well. We get more and more of our drug for less and less effect. It is equally true for maladaptive behaviours because their effect on the brain is exactly the same. We end up with extreme tolerance of our drug or maladaptive behaviour.

Serotonin, on the other hand, does not overexcite, so it does not cause damage. It is something that is good, but we can block it and its effects by overproduction of cortisol caused by stress, pain, hurt, trauma, and addiction. You can't get too much serotonin, but your brain can block its reception and its effects. How does your brain do so? If you have too much dopamine, your brain blocks serotonin.

This is the chemical cause of an idea intrinsic to the 48 Acts: the more pleasure you seek, the more unhappy you become. In a world that is overwhelmed with social media advertising and mainstream marketing of all kinds of stimuli, both chemical and behavioral, it is all too easy to be led astray. It is not your fault. It is the fault of your programming and your early addiction to the most powerful drugs of all: the drugs of approval and appreciation.

You cannot get happiness by taking a substance or engaging in maladaptive behaviours. The problem is that by the time you realize this, you have become addicted to the substance or the maladaptive behaviour in question.

Therefore, you can see how limited medicine and science are to alleviate your addictions, depressions, and maladaptive behaviours, because there is fundamentally very little they can do. They can give you short-term solutions, such as pills to try and build up your serotonin, or many other inhibitors or blockers. Ultimately, though, if serotonin is blocked in your brain due to damage and cortisol, there is very little you can do, and you are trapped. The only way you can alleviate your stress and suffering is to follow the 48 Acts and work out a long-term programme which will, if you follow it, certainly take you from a place of pain to a place of happiness, peace, and contentment. Nothing else can.

ACKNOWLEDGMENTS

I would like to thank a number of people who helped me write this book. I would like to offer my thanks and appreciation: To Robin and Sarah for helping me put this book together in a coherent way. To my wife Maura and my children Sean, Isabelle, Patrick and Alexander for their love and support. To my parents Pat and Anna for life. To all the people from whom I have learned so much. A book like this would not be possible without all who have gone before me. From the earliest hunter gatherers. From Jesus, the Buddha, Aristotle and the Greek philosophers, Hindu sages, Ibn Arabi and the Sufi mystics right up to Nietzsche, Sartre, Merton and countless others. I wish to thank all from whom I have learned and if I have inadvertently omitted any individual please let me know and I will include them in the next edition.

ABOUT THE AUTHOR

Paddy Rafter is a musician, singer, former college lecturer, engineer, academy director and racehorse trainer, husband and father. Paddy has also lived a life of addiction and trauma from an early age and this has led him to many dark places. In the very depths of profound suffering, he fought to find a way out of the hell in which he constantly lived. He discovered a new way to live and to experience the world in peace and happiness. Using this knowledge and experience that he has garnered over a lifetime, he desires to share this with all, so that nobody else should suffer alone, in pain and silence, but use this new way to freedom and joy.

www.paddyrafter.com